How to
Hate Less,
Date Better,
and
Love Always

TRICIA MAXX

Tricia Maxx

The author of this book does not dispense medical advice or prescribe the use of any technique as a form of treatment for physical, emotional, or medical problems without the advice of a physician, either directly or indirectly. The intent of the author is only to offer information of a general nature to help you in your quest for emotional and spiritual well-being. In the event you use any of the information in this book for yourself, which is your constitutional right, the author assumes no responsibility for your actions.

How to Hate Less, Date Better, and Love Always

Table of Contents

Dedication

It goes without saying that my late father inspired me to write this book; if not for him my life would never have been so complicated and interesting. Truly fortunate to have him as my father, I will always cherish the memories and especially the laughs, "88."

Introduction

To be loved is the ultimate validation humans seek. Unlike all things tangible, love cannot be bought and is sometimes never found. During the quest for love we often find ourselves questioning why others behave in such a way that prevents them from falling in love, when we should be trying to solve our own mystery, why are we attracting these individuals?

A relationship blog and a 30-minute spot on television earned me the title of a "cheater expert" and put me in touch with so many who were on the never-ending search to find their soul mate because they believed it held the key to their happiness. I also believed I could solve my problems of being discontent if I met someone, fell in love, got married, and had kids, in that order; but as we write off our failed relationships to be the fault of the other person not playing with a full deck of cards, we must also take comfort in knowing that we are not always dealt the winning hand.

I am going to reveal a part of my life that might make your head spin. If you can keep up, you may have a better understanding of how this book came to be and why I want to share it with you.

My mother abandoned me before my first birthday, returning to Thailand and leaving me behind in Morristown, Tennessee with the only parent I ever came to know, a Southern Caucasian man. I would not discover, until over thirty years later, the man I knew, as "Dad" was not my biological father after all.

I was abused by his family in many ways, including sexually and was called "little nigger," which was confusing because I was raised to believe I was half white.

At the center of my abuse was my grandmother, who when I was an infant, suggested to my father that he leave me on the side of the road like a dog for someone else to pick up and take care of. The abuse started when I had just begun elementary school and worsened as the years went by. Full of anger and feeling hopeless I tried to commit suicide when I was 15.

Around the age of thirty-two I moved to Los Angeles and before I could get settled my dad called to say that my mother had been living in Texas for the past thirty years. She made her way back to the states and married four other men, two of which she had children with. When her eldest son tracked her down seventeen years after she abandoned him, his father broke the silence about her first husband, and me. I was put in contact with my mother and although all I wanted was to know why she never came back to see me being only a five hour plane ride away; what I got was an indistinct story from an alcoholic. She made sure I understood the man who took care of me was not my biological father, but still to this day refuses to disclose whom he is. My life had been one lie after another. To top it off, almost exactly a year after this whirlwind of news, the man who raised me passed away.

For years I would let my past dictate my identity and what kind of "soul mate" I deserved, but that has changed. Accepting I was the common denominator in all of my failed relationships, I took a look at myself and stopped pointing the finger at everyone else. Once I did, I cleared the path to inner peace and happiness.

I am not a therapist or a self-proclaimed relationship expert with a repetitive generic formula to find love. I am a real and imperfect person who encountered obstacles in life many can relate to; living and walking the talk, I am now able to find love on my own terms.

.

Chapter I

Identify Yourself

As far back as I can remember, society played a major role in what I thought I should be, a role that could have lead to my demise. As a child who was bullied in school because of my race, I wanted to be white. I would wear foundation makeup that was about 4 shades too light for my skin and I would lie about my ancestry to offer something more acceptable; I would tell people I was half Cherokee Indian, simply because it was more favored. No matter what the story was, the simple minded people of my hometown only saw what was on the surface so the bullying never ceased.

The things that happened to me as a child were easier to accept because I had no control over them, but the things I did as an adult, the promiscuity and the vile behavior were hard to swallow because I could have said no at any time, but I chose not to. Even the blame I would place on drugs and alcohol would inevitably lead back to the decisions I made as an adult. Though one might believe it is implied within this book, I was not an addict. I was never physically and mentally dependent or unable to stop without incurring adverse effects. I was indeed a substance abuser; I did habitually misuse drugs and alcohol.

Regardless of my past or present, before I could take the first step in getting my life together, I had to come to terms and accept me, in my entirety.

The History of Me

I was conceived somewhere in Thailand, born on an Air Force base in North Carolina. At the time, it was my father's second marriage and my mother's first. My father had retired from the service when we settled down on our family farm in rural Morristown, Tennessee and my first experience with abandonment was underway. To this day I still do not know the truth why when I was nine months old, my mother left to visit her family back in Thailand and never returned to us.

My father who had previously reared four children from his first marriage was left now to be a single parent. With the significant age difference between me and my other siblings, I found myself alone during my adolescent years, but perhaps it was for the best.

My father and I lived in a single wide trailer that we made a poor attempt at disguising as a house by adding a shingled roof and vinyl siding; it was in such poor condition, one day I fell through the floor in the hallway. Our yard was ridiculously full of trash. I would often make my friends drop me off up the road so they wouldn't see where I lived. To say the least, my family was dysfunctional. As many families in the rural south, we had our share of welfare recipients, small business owners, churchgoers and backsliders, but unlike most, we had a little half-breed who became the reason her family felt each carried a dark secret.

As a child, my understanding was I was of mixed race with my father being Caucasian and my mother, Asian. My confusion set in when I started kindergarten and the children hurled the slur "nigger" at me. When I heard my relatives say the word it was directed towards black people and I wasn't black, or so I thought.

Even my relatives would call me the repugnant racial slur. I recall a summer afternoon while out on a walk with my cousins and my grandmother's brother, one of my younger cousins slipped out of her shoes to walk barefoot; as we walked she dropped one. When I squatted down to pick it up for her, my grandmother's brother shouted, "You'd better get your shoe before that little nigger gets it!" I was only six years old and being called a derogatory racial slur by a grown man.

Grandma Dearest

One of my most horrific childhood memories took place when I was around eight years old or so. It was a day when my grandmother called me outside to help her while she killed some chickens for dinner. When I went outside she made me stand still while she wrung their necks until their heads came off and then threw their headless bodies at me, their bodies flailed about while blood spewed from their necks onto my legs and she just stood there laughing as I cried.

Around age twelve, my father began a job that started him working at 3:00am. Unable to personally ensure I would keep with my school schedule he sent me to live with her. This was when my nightmare truly began. I am not entirely sure why, but it was obvious my grandmother loathed me. She was the typical bigoted hypocrite, so I can assume it had something to do with my race, and she knew I wasn't a blood relative. She was emotionally and physically abusive, and turned a blind eye to those who were sexually inappropriate with me. My father would later tell me he would routinely visit my grandmother's house and would have to dig my schoolbooks and homework from her trashcan where she dumped them while I slept.

Finding it hard to cope with the pain at age fifteen, I made a failed attempt at suicide. Due to my relative young age and being unable to gain access to sleeping pills, I found and took an entire box of maximum strength cold medication. Surviving the night, I awakened in the morning to my grandmother's habitual screeching and a crippling headache.

She passed away when I was nineteen and for some reason, I was sad. Never understood why, as I never felt loved by her. Perhaps it was only the kind of sadness death brings. Or perhaps I thought our relationship was how we were supposed to treat the ones we loved? I fortunately had friends in high school during that time that loved me and would always come to my rescue.

In high school, while a true supporter of 80s fashion and hair, I went through an identity crisis. I was a trendsetter, always wearing some hideously designed spandex, my face was slathered with a ton of makeup, and I had blue streaks in my hair. I always thought of myself as an outcast who fitted in; a lot of my friends were rebels, while many of my other friends were part of the in-crowd.

One of the saddest things about high school was that only a few teachers encouraged me to be unique, while others encouraged the bullying for it. I remember my high school science teacher ridiculing me in class over my hairstyle. Apparently, he didn't find it attractive and thought it was appropriate to make fun of me in front of my classmates, but when I would respond by pointing out his early set male pattern baldness I would be the one to get reprimanded. I often wonder how my life might have been different had he made an effort to find out if my identity was just me being a kid or if it were perhaps a cry for help, rather than just writing me off as a weirdo.

Today, a lot of my high school friends say looking back, they always knew I was going to be the one who left the small hick town we called home and never come back. Just one week and three days after I graduated high school, that's exactly what I did.

Rock Bottom

A mere $3000 cash in hand may be a sign of balling in Tennessee, however, in The City of Angels; it is a paycheck away from poverty. I set out for Los Angeles right after high school. Within three weeks I was running home to the comfort of daddy. Stubbornness made me determined not to stay home, so I moved to Washington, DC for a short time, but falling on my butt again, I decided to give Atlanta a try.

If you are not familiar with the attraction of Atlanta, allow me to familiarize you. Upon setting foot on Peachtree Street, I was in awe of the nightlife, the 24-hour clubs, accessible celebrities and a southern state where the practice of racism was laxed. Before I knew it, I was dating men of another race, which was taboo in the small town where I was from.

The first black man I dated was an NFL rookie who went on to become one of the leading receivers for the Pittsburgh Steelers. Before long, every guy I dated was some sort of "baller"; my definition of dating at the time was actually known as a "booty call." As a matter of fact, by the end of my early 20's I had slept with more men than most do in a lifetime. I believed my behavior to stem from the naivety of a simple small town girl, but it was indeed something far worse.

My behavior caught up with me when I had a fling with a well-known R&B artist. He flew me around the US and even took me on tour with him. It was like living the dream and I had even become pregnant with his child. The fairy tale ended after I barely escaped with my life after being rushed to the emergency room with a ruptured ectopic pregnancy. He offered no help, no condolences, and absolutely no emotional support. I later learned that he boasted about the affair and how he treated the situation.

I was so angry, so lonely and felt so unloved; my only consolation was the nightlife. I started going out to the clubs every night they were open. I made friends with the club owners, so I always got the VIP treatment and never had to stand in the long lines. The attention and special treatment made me feel wanted and validated. I made many friends quickly, but unfortunately many of them were drug dealers.

During my club-going days, I began masking my pain with cocaine and ecstasy. Pretty soon, I developed a cocaine habit that kept me from paying rent and car payments. My car was repossessed and I was evicted from home twice. I became homeless. Couch surfing and living in extended stay hotels became the norm to me.

I eventually ended up apartment sitting at a complex located in a high crime area off Campbellton Road in Atlanta. Running with lowlifes, I found myself shot at numerous times and a gun once forced into my mouth. Feeling my life was increasingly becoming more and more out of control, I broke down one day and sought refuge again with my father. In retrospect, it's interesting how the one place I desperately fled ended up being the same place I sought shelter.

Change

Returning home to spend time with my dad and away from the club scene, I was finally beginning to think clearly. I did not go through an enlightening experience or an "ah ha" moment, but I realized if I were to return to Atlanta, the best thing to do was sever contact with most of the so called friends I had made. When I gave the city another chance, I was ready. I got my life together with the basic necessities needed to live on my own and though I did not return to drugs, unfortunately, I did return to the nightlife.

Soon, I found myself right back at the bars, hamming it up with celebrities and the high rollers, just like old times and since I was able maintain what I had regained, I thought I was in control; but I was still angry, lonely, and feeling unloved. These poignant feelings I could not shake eventually led to more drinking and promiscuity, which escalated to bar fights with women and even men believe it or not. Nothing had changed in my behavior and I found myself searching for the bottom again. I needed real change. I needed a new start and Los Angeles was calling.

When I touched down in Los Angeles this time, I finally felt free. I was away from all the racism, the aggressive men and a life full of never ending troubles. Being open-minded my entire life, the transition to fitting in was easy however, one thing I was not accustomed to was the flaky mentality of the Angelinos.

I thought I had hit the jackpot when I found a job opportunity through the internet before even moving. However, after moving across the country and registering for a work permit at the request of the manager, the owners decided to give the position to someone within the company without even the decency of a courtesy call. It was a harsh and unlucky blow that would seem to put my world in upheaval. I quickly had to move from my beautiful Studio City apartment and relocate to the sketchy, seedy suburb of Reseda.

Refusing to fail again and after only a couple weeks of networking I landed a job in Pasadena. I seemed to blend right in as I was surrounded by so many of different ethnicity, mostly Asian. This time no one asked where I was from because of the way I looked – they asked because of my southern twang. I started feeling great about my decision to move and everything was falling into place. It finally seemed as though my future was bright and my past was in the rear view mirror, or so I thought...

It was my seventh month as a California resident when I received some shocking news. It was a Memorial Day afternoon when my father called for what I thought was a routine "hello," but I would soon realize it was more than that. I could hear it in the long pauses he took in between words. There was no easy way to say what he'd heard, so he was blunt.

"Patricia, your mother is alive and has been living in Texas for the last thirty years."

Here I am, getting adjusted to my new life and the past comes rushing back at me. Apparently, as it turned out, within a year after my mother retreated back to Thailand she found another American in the military to marry and made her way back to the United States. As a matter of fact, she had been married three times since leaving my father without ever getting divorced from him.

Here is where it begins to get complicated; my mother and her second husband had a son and when they divorced, she abandoned him as well. She stayed in contact with him for some time, but soon grew estranged when he was only ten years old. Now twenty-seven, he was about to become a father when he began his search for the woman he longed to make the grandmother of his child. In his search, he found the woman that had once been a mother to him and when he found her, he also found her secret, that she had abandoned her first child – her daughter – years ago in Tennessee.

Upon receiving the news I became overwhelmed with emotions and bombarded by an influx of unsolicited advice on how I should handle myself. There were so many eager to see how the situation would play out without any sensitivity for how I was being affected emotionally.

Not one person asked how I felt about the news; all they wanted to know was when I planned to meet her. Clearly, they had seen too many family reunions on daytime television.

Just like that, with only a forty-five minute phone call from my father my life and what I knew of it would forever change. Until that moment I had lived my life with the fantasies I'd created of my mom being dead, in prison, or a part of some life threatening government conspiracy because I couldn't think of any other possible reason she would just vanish. Most of the abandonment situations I had been exposed to by others was when the father was absent, not the mother. I had never really put much thought into the notion that a mother would be as capable of doing such a thing.

Nonetheless, I gave my mother two chances at having a presence in my life. The first time we connected she confirmed the man I called "Dad" was not my biological father. My biological father played a role in her explanation as to why she left so many years ago; he was the man she left me behind to reunite with. She refused to tell me his name and insisted that who he was didn't matter. The only information she would divulge was that I looked like him.

The half story left with more unknowns was certainly a lot to process. Unfortunately, my mother did not understand how the circumstances affected me and after her third drunken message for not returning her call in a timely manner, I cut off contact indefinitely.

Shortly after I spoke to my mother for the first time, the man I called Dad suddenly died of a pulmonary embolism. I had spoken to him earlier in the day before he passed and he seemed fine; I can still hear his voice and the puzzling question he asked before we said good-bye forever, "Were you just calling to let me know you were going to be okay?"

After two years of grieving, I felt it was time to give my mother another chance since I had taken some time to reassess the overall situation and process the chain of events. My only dilemma was that I no longer had a way to get in contact with her. She had gotten a divorce from her fourth husband and her whereabouts were unknown. Additionally, her eldest son had taken an interest in how much money I stood to inherit when my father passed, but when I made it clear it wasn't going to affect him in anyway, meaning he wouldn't see any of it, he disappeared as well.

This left me with the only other option at the time, which was to find my younger brothers. Fortunately, knowing the trends of the twenty year olds I had a strong feeling I would be able to locate my younger brothers on Facebook, the only problem was I didn't know their last names. After several months of investigating my own mother, I figured it out and my very first search put me into direct contact with my youngest brother.

It was an awkward email, but I was as blunt as the man who raised me and simply said, "This might be a bit odd, but you may know who I am, I'm your sister." He immediately wrote back and expressed how delighted he was to hear from me.

He and my other brother had been searching for me, but were told not to contact me by their older brother. They were told I was on the verge of suicide and any contact from them would push me over the edge, none of which was true. They were fed the story to deter them from contacting me.

Apparently, soon after the eldest son reunited with our mother, he inflicted a financial burden upon her he didn't want me to know about. The special interest he had in how much money I stood to inherit confirmed what my gut had been telling me about him, he was bad news.

My little brothers on the other hand, were nothing like him and I was surprised by the connection we had. While first speaking to them on a conference call I felt as if they had always been around and it wasn't the first time I had heard their voices. It was like talking to old friends you just hadn't heard from in a while. Perhaps when I'd found out about them years before, they were always around in my heart.

When I connected with my mother the second time, I didn't know what to expect, so all I could do was explain why I severed contact and tell her how I felt about the way things were progressing in my life and my hopes for the future. She seemed to understand and explained that she too was overwhelmed by it all and had also gone through some drastic changes in her life as a result of what happened.

After that day, we called each other often and I thought for a moment we might be able to have a decent mother/daughter relationship, but I was only setting myself up to be disappointed, again.

After only a few weeks of talking, my mother and I decided it was time to meet in person. This was something I never dreamt would happen, since all my dreams of my mother were that she was dead or unavailable. For me, I anticipated this meeting; after all, it was my mother. I would finally see what she looked like and see if I resembled her in any way and I had so many questions. Sadly, she was very, very, cavalier about meeting me.

We made arrangements twice for her to come to Los Angeles and after I had taken off work she simply wouldn't confirm and I wouldn't hear from her for weeks. When I would finally hear from her she would say that she only had 2 days of vacation and then the 2 days would turn into 2 weeks. My younger brother was going to pay for her trip, but she could never keep her story straight thus made it impossible to make a solid plan. She later called hinting around she wanted to move to Los Angeles and live with me. She inquired about jobs and what my living situation was like. I could easily see that she was intending to put me on her list of enablers, but I had to be strong and walk away. The decision I made to walk away wasn't out of spite; I wasn't going to be responsible for a dysfunctional adult when I had my own issues to address.

I haven't had any contact with my mother since then and that was back in 2009, but I still keep in contact with my younger brothers, with exception to her oldest son. I haven't met either of them, but I certainly plan to. From time to time I ask about our mother, but not surprisingly, they have nothing pleasant to report as they seldom hear from her and often do not know her whereabouts.

I didn't have the past one would boast about being wonderful that was filled with the love of a family with a strong bond, but it was indeed my life whether I liked it or not. For years it played a distinctive role in the way I viewed an approached my relationships with people and my love life. I was ashamed of who I was. I thought the best thing to do was to make up stories about my parents and childhood because of the shame. I was afraid the men I dated would harshly judge and be embarrassed to be associated with me.

I have learned that one has to be honest with themselves and others about who they are in order to truly move forward and make the changes needed to contribute to a healthy relationship. Otherwise, it is just a dream we are selling and we all eventually wake from dreams; and that is when our "true self" will emerge.

Desperate

Being desperate is often viewed as a sign of weakness. Who wants to known as someone with the emotional state of mind of a person who feels as if they're left with no options, or someone being forced to make irrational decisions and is more willing to accept what is available to them despite it being against their preference? When it comes to saving a life, it's okay to be desperate it seems, but when it comes to romance, it is almost always a turn off.

The desperate usually have a distorted view of themselves. When they play mind games with others they see themselves as conquerors, completely oblivious to the fact that they have to result to such tactics because they are lacking what is desired to lure or capture the interest of another naturally.

Desperation pressures one to buy into the many " dating theories" offered by the hundreds of "self-proclaimed relationship experts," one recommendation for such theories often suggests changing oneself simply to attract someone. The changes can include altering their faces or body, changing their style, and indulging in activities they normally would avoid. For instance, many women who have no interest in sports will hang out in sports bars because it is usually where the men are.

The most absurd "theory" I have ever heard was a suggestion to show cleavage because men like breasts and seeing them triggers a need to be nurtured, therefore, I would appear to be a nurturer and more men would be attracted to me. Sadly, people are misled by advice from the so-called experts who don't even know the difference between a hypothesis and a theory.

Placing yourself outside your comfort zone might be counterproductive. It is often difficult to relax and be yourself when you are uncomfortable, which tends to give off a vibe, which might imply you're not having a good time and that can make you appear unapproachable.

Perhaps the reason the divorce rate is so high is because many attract one another by pretending to be something they're not? I have met many men and women and know some personally, who are going through a divorce, getting divorced again (some even getting divorced again from the same person), or wishing they were divorced. Many pity me for being single and unmarried at age 40, but while I may have never been married, I have also never been divorced. I do realize that at my age and living in Los Angeles I should be on at least my second husband!

Needy

Despite all my childhood issues, I am a true nurturer. I am constantly taking care of others; nurturing extends to animals, plants, the homeless, and the elderly. Because of this, I mostly attract men who need to be taken care of emotionally and even financially. This type of man is far from what I am attracted to. The people and things I help cannot help themselves and I don't expect them to be able to give back to me. When it comes to a romance, I expect someone to be able to give as much as they take or it isn't going to work for me. I have come to this conclusion after several failed relationships in which I tried to fix the other person, always being the one who rescued others while completely depriving myself of my own needs. Needs, being the security in knowing that if I should fall down, the man I am with is strong enough to pick me up; and knowing I can fall into the abyss he will take care when wiping my tears with true understanding.

This doesn't mean I look down on those who are not self-reliant in a relationship. Again, another negative dictated by society is the label of *needy and clingy*. If a person *needs* to be told they're the object of ones desire they're considered needy. If for whatever reason they can't comprehend what most would consider simple instruction without a consultation with their significant other, they're considered needy. For example, a young man I once courted would call me during the middle of the day to ask where he could purchase red candles. Aside from not using the internet to search places to shop he could have entered any random drugstore and found these items. At first I thought he was just looking for an excuse to call me, but then later after a few more dates it became apparent that he wasn't a self-starter, he was lazy and unmotivated. This type of behavior doesn't work for me. When a guy hears this he immediately thinks I am insensitive and hard, however, the reason it doesn't work is because I am what they call a **career woman**. I simply don't have the lifestyle that meets the needs of someone who requires constant contact and attention. Being busy working on projects, meetings in different time zones, and just being too tired at the end of the day to do anything but send a text "good-nite love" actually does happen in real life with no hidden meanings.

It may come as a surprise, but there are actually those who desire someone they can support and nurture. There are others who want to be the recipient of constant attention and endless contact throughout the day. It is all about perspective and what works for others. In the end, their needs are being met. One has to be completely honest with what their needs are regardless of being judged by others.

Unavailable

Commitment phobic is generally thrown in the way of those who are in a relationship, but are not fully available; an "absentee" if you will. They're unavailable to put the time into a relationship, time most would consider to be normal. The masses tend to believe the lack of time is due to fear of committing. If the commitment phobic individual doesn't show up as often there is less chance of he or she committing to one person, or so they say. For example, if you are dating someone and you spend several days during the week together then it might appear as if you are interested in a committed relationship. Whereas, if you see someone every now and then, but you drag it out over several months, it looks as if the interest is there, however you are not committing your time. The reality of both scenarios is #1. If someone doesn't want to be in a commitment, they can see you every day and still not commit. #2. Someone might want a commitment, but not have the time to see you every day- but they are okay with that as long as they see you-some time is better than no time. Sometimes this has more to do with someone being a workaholic and nothing to do with the lack of invested interest in the other person. Many often say when you meet the right person you will make time for them, which is true, but quality time is also based on perspective.

Another version of being commitment phobic or just being someone who has "issues" is when you are a man or a woman of a certain age an still single. It is said that a commitment will cramp ones style or that he or she refuses to grow up and grow old. How about this one? There is a lot of freedom with being single. Not meaning, freedom to sleep around and be a serial dater, freedom to come and go as you wish and do what you want without your decisions hurting or affecting anyone.

When people ask me if I'm available, I often reply, "Available for what?" There are a lot of things someone might need in a relationship and I can't guarantee I am available for all those things. "Am I available to meet your needs?" Might be a better question.

Conforming to the wants and needs of what others want in a desperate attempt to find love means you are being dishonest. You are not being honest with yourself and you are not being honest with the person you desire. Though you might want something long term, you are luring someone under false pretenses and this is merely a road to a temporary relationship. Your true self will come out eventually and the person you have "hooked" may leave because you have shattered their expectations or they simply find your true self incompatible. You will have wasted their time and yours.

For our ego's sake, we try to disguise this as compromising, but it's not having compromise the relationship if you are letting go of your true identity.

Ready

Most of my adult life I have known people who often say they want to be in a relationship, but yet they're always open to the next best thing that comes along once they're in one. They say it's because they need variety and something to compare to what they have in order to appreciate it more. These are the words of people who are discontent. Usually if one is discontent in their relationship they are probably the same way in other aspects of life. They are never satisfied. For example, someone who has the newest version of their favorite car, but they continuously look forward to the next upgrade or newer model's features.

For years I longed for a relationship that would eventually lead to marriage, but I was never ready. Even when I was 24 years old, I could have married a famous actor and never have had to work again, but inside I thought, "If I marry him, I can't go out with so and so if I should meet them one day."

I believe I am ready, but some still insist the "universe" doesn't believe I am, thus why I am still single. They act as if the choice to be single is not mine. Most who feel this way have a very traditional way of thinking when it comes to marriage and most of them are married. They believe the way you should be married or the steps toward making the move in that direction should mirror the way they did it.

The Playette

There was a time when there were so many men in my life that my friends couldn't keep up with their names. Instead, they would refer to them by the part of town in which the men lived. Oddly, I wanted something meaningful so I wouldn't date them during the same time so there would be no overlap. I would get to know one and if he wasn't what I was looking for then I moved on to the next. I found this to be the only way to give someone a fair chance because I was giving them my undivided attention. For me, dating several men at once took up a lot of time because I had to divide my time between those several and it prolonged the process of determining if someone was compatible.

I found that some men placed a lot of importance on the length of time I kept them in my life, rather than the actual time they spent with me, especially when I ended up breaking it off with them. Having someone around for a month or so can make one believe it is "going somewhere," and when they are abruptly cut loose they can become really confused and often feel led on.

It takes me roughly about four dates to know if someone is worth pursuing for something serious. The first date I can tell if he is a kind person. Some will argue that it doesn't matter how well others are treated as long as YOU are treated well. I disagree completely. The way one treats others is a direct reflection of them. Anyone can be nice to you on the first few dates, but if they are unkind in general then pretty soon you will become one of the many who are subject to their behavior. If someone treats the service staff poorly or tries to show they're in charge by speaking sternly when it isn't warranted, that's a sign of an angry or bitter person. Definitely doesn't work for me.

On the second date, we're a little more comfortable so the jokes come out and the guard starts to come down. If he didn't make any racist or other offensive comments then we will probably make it to date #3.

On the third date, we have probably engaged in texting or in depth phone conversations beforehand, so this is when the real him starts to come out. I can usually tell if he wants a compatible partner, or if he needs professional help. I'm not saying that to be funny. Most of the third dates have been when they've unloaded their problems for you to solve or to listen to. You have to take note to how old these problems are. This is important. If it's something that just happened today or during the week, it is probably just something for dinner conversation. If the problems are months or years old, then this person is not making adjustments or taking steps to improve the situation, but is simply going to complain about it day in and day out. This can be very exhausting.

If we make it to the fourth date we probably have enough in common to want to see each other again and he doesn't seem to have any of the major personality flaws I dislike. It is a scary thing, but I have been on first dates in which a man was rude to the server, made racist comments about Asians (trying to be funny,) and unloaded his grief about what a tyrant his employer was and how he hated him. That date lasted about 15 minutes.

Chapter II

Tribulations

Exes

Some relationships end on good notes with both individuals walking away in a friendly manner. This usually happens when the couple reaches that point in their relationship when they just know it's not working. No one is to blame; the spark just isn't there. While others have explosive endings. Someone cheated, someone lost that loving feeling long ago, but left the other one hanging with no direction or any number of terrible things. Whichever way it ended, it can be painfully obvious when someone still has feelings for the ex. There are subtle signs and blatant gestures we notice every day, but we choose to ignore for the sake of staying in a relationship that will inevitably be riddled with heartache and chaos, just because we like the way it sounds to say "we're seeing someone."

When I get to the point of being comfortable enough with someone to spend time with them in their home, the last thing I want to see are photos of the ex lying around. Granted, I still have vacation photos with my ex in my possession, but they are in a box in the top of my closet. One might ask why I kept them? The answer is pretty simple; they are a collection of a time in my life when I went to an amazing place. They are not in a photo album on the center of my coffee table.

I was in the second or third month of dating this guy I'd met through a similar interest group. We had been on several dinner dates, seen movies, and gone to a few conventions. One night we decided to dine at a posh Brazilian restaurant not far from his home. The atmosphere was cozy and the food was divine. It was by far one of the best dinner dates we'd had, until he said, "My ex-girlfriend and I used to come here all the time." What in the ---- did he just say to me? I shrugged it off. Maybe he liked the food so much he wasn't thinking. It wasn't that big of a deal at first until he followed with, "My ex-girlfriend was Brazilian and a real looker." Now I'm thinking, he must be trying to break it off and maybe because of his lack of communication skills this is how he feels is the best way?

We later stopped by his house so he could show me his progress on a project he was working on. I took at seat in the living room while he went away to the kitchen to get some water for us. As I looked down I noticed a beautiful coffee table with a rather large photo album in the center of it. Obviously, it was placed on display for visitors to take a looksee, so that's what I did. The photo album was filled with 8x10 photos from his vacation with his ex from **ten** years ago and photos of her as well...

Did I become jealous when I saw these photos? Not at all. but, I was definitely turned off and less confused. He was holding a torch for this woman for ten years. It was really sad, he could not let her go and I believe it is the real reason all his relationships thereafter failed. He could not let go, therefore he could not move on.

The next few encounters I had with potential suitors that would at some point include repeated mentioning of the ex, I would simply say "good-bye, here's why." When everything reminds them of the ex, from places they go, things they smell, or situations they encounter, I feel as if they're still holding on and not ready to move on with me. At times they even compare us to the ex without thinking and without realizing they are doing more harm than good by pointing out our similarities.

Once in a while a situation might present itself that is specific to the ex. For example, if you are discussing going on vacation together and THEY mention Hawaii and you say you've been already and you are asked who you were with and it just so happens to be your ex! Or if there is information that no one on the planet would know except your ex, but this should not be every day or every other day. Some argue being bothered by the ex is a sign of insecurity and jealousy, maybe so, however, I tend to look at it this way; the ex is an ex for a reason, therefore, if he is currently with me even though I am so much like his ex, he must not have learned his lesson the first time around and must be a glutton for punishment. In the case that he has been dumped and he is looking to replace his ex with me because I'm again, so much like her, he is not ready and I am a mere rebound.

Almost all my exes tried to reconcile with me when they felt it was time to stop being a player and time to settle down. Regardless, we hadn't had any contact in several months or even years, they were ready to give me the house with the white picket fence that I longed for in the past and each had their own version of the same speech:

> "Hey girl, haven't heard from you in a while. Just calling to see how you were doing. I've been thinking about us a lot lately. This might sound crazy, but I realized how great you were and you are definitely the one I want to be the mother of my children."

It really had nothing to do with what a great person I was, it was all about reproducing their offspring. After being offended, I politely declined. They of course, went on to the next girl in their contacts until they found someone who said, "Yes." Within about 6 months, the lucky girls where saying, "I do."

Another only wanted me to have his child without actually marrying me. His decision wasn't based on my character at all; it was based solely on my DNA! His opinion was that I had the superior DNA that would be ideal for the child he wanted to create. Determined to be a father he became relentless with his request and assured me that I wouldn't have to have any responsibility for "it" when it was born, unless I wanted to. When I suggested adopting a baby, his reply was, *"I don't want some other person's reject."* He actually thought I would want to have a baby with someone who could refer to a baby as a reject, while at the same time he was fully aware that I was, for all intents and purposes, adopted. This was such a poor choice of words considering he knew the situation with my parents. I told him I was thankful my father did not share his view of raising "some other person's reject," and let him go.

Some people are marriage minded from the moment they have their first kiss and up until they say, "I do." Others never are, never were, and probably never will.

Cheaters

I am known for having dated many cheaters, and for the longest time I believed I was the cause of their behavior, but I educated myself and what I found was highly valuable to my self-healing.

Almost everyone has been cheated on whether they know it or not or they have cheated. I believe this is why we feel there is a need to know the psychology behind cheating. When I was cheated on, the first thing I wanted to know was who the "other woman" was. What did she look like first and foremost? What does she do for a living? Who is she? These questions popped into my mind simply because I wanted to know why she was better than me. After all, why would he have strayed unless it was to upgrade right? What I found was, some of the men weren't physically attracted more to the other women, nor did they believe they had a higher status, they just thought they were more pleasant to be around than me and in some cases it was none of the above, they just did it because they couldn't say no to another woman. I want to be clear that I am in no way condoning the cheaters behavior.

Yes, it is possible that a cheater might stray because they feel the person they are attached to is unbearable. Here is the thing about that; they have the option to leave. So here comes the tricky part. What makes them stay and then cheat?

When I hear theories about why the cheater cheats, I find most of the time many are just making excuses for bad behavior. Many who say men cheat because it's in their DNA are actual cheaters themselves; they free themselves from responsibility by blaming biology rather than being held accountable for their infidelity. They often refer to the anthropological tale of the man sowing as many seeds as he can to ensure preservation of his bloodline, meaning fathering many children.

However, if this were really the case why do so many cheating men take precautions not to get the "other woman" pregnant? I believe it is best to phrase this as men having urges; however, we all have urges but we don't always act upon them nor are we forced to.

Men are not the only cheaters. Historically, women cheated less because they didn't have the freedom to easily do so however, they still cheated. In seventeenth century England, legal records reflect a high count of infidelity by women.

When a person cheats it has nothing to do with the person they're cheating on, but more to do with how he or she feels about them. They are often unhappy in their relationship, but a sense of low self-worth keeps them from walking away from their unhappy situation. Many say they love the person they are with but the person is lacking something which is why they strayed, this diverts the blame away from them and onto the person they're cheating on. The bottom line is it's his or her choice to handle the situation with some integrity, or to cheat.

There are signs of cheater potential. Sorry to say that I disagree that you can tell if someone is a cheater simply by their outer appearance. Some experts suggest that certain areas in which a cheater's hands are positioned, shifty eyes, or risqué attire means "cheater." Here is what I have to offer on that hypothesis: Politicians are well groomed, well dressed, and well mannered. Have you ever known a politician to cheat? I thought so.

In a random survey I conducted that was circulated via Facebook, I found that most of the men who cheated and blamed biology for the reason had a female following online. The women did not appear to be family or distant relatives, at least not from the comments they were posting, and their male to female ratio of friends favored the females. The most interesting thing about it was that these men also argue there aren't any "good women" left in the world, but yet they have so many female friends.

The women who cheated were the opposite. They had photos of themselves posted with mostly gal pals and hardly any male friends. They claimed to have cheated because the person they cheated with was an upgrade from the person they were in a relationship with. They were able to provide better things for them. Some of those things included fine dining, vacations, and more financial freedom.

Of the cheaters I dated most were flirts and most of the flirtatious men I know or knew personally are cheaters or have cheated. Flirtatious cheaters often flirt with others within their dating spectrum to see if there is a chance; though they claim they are just being friendly they will also disguise the flirtation as a mere compliment. If it were necessary to flirt while offering a compliment wouldn't everyone be doing it?

Sometimes cheating is a result from experiencing *covert incest,* also known as *emotional incest.* Emotional incest is when a parent expects a child to fulfill their emotional needs without actually having sexual contact. Aside from all the emotional scarring, when the child becomes an adult, he or she has the potential to become a sex addict, as sex becomes a coping mechanism for obstacles in life, including their relationship disputes.

This would be the only time I find the explanation of cheating to be in a person's nature plausible; however, it is a reason, not an excuse. Part of being an adult is having the freedom to think and make choices on our own.

There are many reasons why a cheater cheats. Unfortunately, we are all too often willing to accept a superficial excuse.

Cheating on Facebook

Social media has been one of the most common methods used to catch someone in the act of cheating. Most of the avid Facebook users tend to put details of their entire lives on display, from what they had to lunch to the random thought that just crossed their minds, or they check themselves in to places because they want everyone to know.

Though many refer to cheating as mainly an act of sex or other physically romantic encounter, *the definition of cheating is: to trick or deceive.* So, does it mean you are cheating if you carry on a private online relationship if there was no physical contact? I feel it does. Though no sex was involved, the emotions are the same during the interaction and your partner will still feel betrayed so it's all the same to me.

There have been times when I have searched for my exes online to see how they were doing or if they were still alive. I did it out of simple curiosity and I was not in a relationship at the time. Some seek out their exes because they're still holding onto something and they want to either stir trouble or see if there is a tiny bit of something felt by the ex that could spark or rekindle a romance. Another reason is that they want to gloat and show their ex how great their life turned out without them, but this proves they're still holding on because the ex's opinion is sought.

Unfortunately, it may be hard to tell what someone's motives are. I have been in situations when a networking or business opportunity was actually a way to pry the door back open to test the waters. One of my exes was an actor and needed some headshots so he called one day to see what my rates were since being a professional photographer was something I did. After about 15 minutes of business discussion the conversation shifted into inquires about my personal life and suggestive sexual comments. I could see right away that he really wasn't interested in headshots; he was interested in me.

I was dating someone who thought it would be harmless to become online friends with a gal he dated. Little did he know she would later attempt "befriend" every girl he dated and even went so far as to contact me. She took it upon herself to reassure me that she was of no threat to me and said she didn't understand why I didn't like her. She claimed that the person I was dating, her ex, told her this information. Of course it was a half-truth. Still, it was totally unnecessary for her to contact me and it was a bit creepy I might add.

In the past I've discovered someone I was dating had been contacting an ex whom he knew I would not approve of and lied to me about it when it happened. To clarify the reason I would not approve: This person had already played the typical two-faced catty female role to me. You know, the one when they act like every thing is over and they think you're great and they are so happy for the two of you and then they turn around and say the complete opposite to others? The reason he contacted her was innocent, but it was the lying that killed our relationship. If it was just a call, no harm no foul, but as it turned out they had planned to meet for coffee one day to discuss a business opportunity, or so he says. I didn't want to be with a liar. Whether or not you are with a liar depends on what you want in your relationship. I didn't want to be with someone I could never trust. Questioning whether or not every word that comes out of their mouth is a lie is a drag.

How to catch a cheater

The best way to catch a cheater is by listening to your gut instinct; however, it can be tricky especially for someone who is a true pessimist. If someone doesn't answer the phone the first time they call they immediately assume the reason is because they are tied up, or in bed with someone else. When in reality, there are a number of reasons why their call was missed. Cell phones aren't the most reliable and you sure can't take one into the shower with you.

Then you have others who refuse to trust their instincts. Sometimes we are presented with a situation that just feels wrong, but we apply foolish optimism and get sorely disappointed. You know someone is being unfaithful, but you will justify his or her story and even add your own "truth" to it just to put yourself at ease.

Here are some example behaviors of the cheaters I dated. Please keep in mind, I'm not saying if a man is doing these things it means he's cheating, I'm just saying these are some of the things my cheaters did.

My cheaters:

I would often find girlie belongings like hairpins, toiletries, and lipstick on glasses around their homes. When I would confront them their first reaction would be, "Why are you snooping around my house?" This was a sign of guilt right off the bat. First of all, they **assumed** I was snooping, which indicates that they knew about these items and hid them. Secondly, you know you don't really have to snoop. When "the other woman" is with the man they plant things for other women to find. After I would point out that these items were left in plain sight, their second reaction would be, *"If I were cheating, I wouldn't leave things out in the open for you to see. I'm not stupid."* This is a pretty common use of reverse psychology that the naive fall for.

A couple of the cheaters did not spend the night at my house nor would they invite me to stay over at theirs. In this instance, unbeknown to me, I was the other woman. Understand, I thought I was being cheated on, but it was the other way around. One of the men was engaged the entire time, what an unlucky girl his fiancé was.

Another cheater changed his bed sheets at least three times a week. Do you know any man who does this? Even the neatest neat freak doesn't do this. This guy wasn't mysophobic either. Some say he did it out of respect for me? Respect? He was cheating, so how in any way was this respectful. Changing the sheets so that I don't sleep in some other woman's biological residue is a very small gesture when compared to what happened beforehand.

I drove myself crazy when I stayed with someone after I caught them cheating. I would be at their home, always on the lookout for evidence. Doing this made me feel dirty and disgusted for not loving myself enough to do better to just leave someone behind who didn't respect me and someone I didn't trust.

Now, I won't give a second chance to a cheater, once the deed is done, it's over and he's out for good. Sometimes men are actually capable of realizing they've made a mistake and are afraid of losing something good forever and probably would never cheat again, but I personally cannot trust someone again once the trust is broken, plus cross contamination makes me nervous with all the STDs out there. A lot of married couples compromise on this to save the marriage especially when children are involved, I'm not sure that I would. Hats off to them for being able to get over it with that memory burned into their brain.

The Drama Queen

"Oh what a drama queen!" I'm sure you have heard someone say it at one time or another. I will admit to inflicting my fair share of drama in the past when I've "reacted" to a situation. When it comes to wearing this crown, everyone else is a drama queen, but not us right? Who are the ones who love the drama? Is it the person who confronts those who are involved when a shady situation has been discovered, or is it the party that created the actual shady situation itself? There will always be someone who says, "I do not want to get involved in your drama," but then they are the first in line to discuss it.

I have never denied someone I was dating from being on friendly terms with their ex. I think it's healthy for people to be friends, granted everyone has moved on. I said before, being friends with an ex can be tricky because you really don't know what their motives are. Sometimes they're not carrying a torch, but they just like to be disruptive by projecting their failed relationships onto yours.

A few years ago, a guy I was dating had an ex who coincidentally was dating someone I knew 20 years ago. She and her guy were basically two untrusting peas in one dysfunctional pod and because we were all connected on Facebook through mutual friends, somehow I got in the middle of their tangled web of shadiness. Her man contacted me under the false pretense of "reconnecting with old friends." In reality he contacted me to pump me for information about the guy I was dating and to see if it would somehow give him the answers he needed. Apparently, my long lost friend had fallen out with this woman, I guess he wanted some sort of closure and thought I could tell him something to make him feel better. The entire situation became so twisted that I ended up severing contact with my long lost friend because his behavior seemed a bit too obsessive and creepy.

The woman passed her number to another mutual friend to give to me; she wanted me to call her to tell me her side of the story and ask what transpired with her man. Seemed a reasonable request. I ended up befriending her. She would text and call me to lay out her issues and seek advice. I thought we had started a genuine friendship. She invited me to see her perform at some of the local venues in Los Angeles and I went!

Earlier on in my relationship I mentioned to my guy that I thought it was great that she and I were friends, but later when we split he wanted to show me that I was a fool. I will assume by proving that I was manipulated would somehow give him "the win." He wanted to show me how I got fooled by her fake friendship and forwarded me several sections of their email correspondence in which she stated that she really didn't like me and called me a drama queen. She also suggested he kept their conversations a secret. In fact, if I saw her number on our phone bill he should tell me they were talking about something else. Basically, she was requesting my boyfriend (at the time) to lie to me, knowing it would compromise the trust in our relationship.

I believe boundaries are necessary when it comes to the level of communication we have with our exes in order to maintain respect and peace with our partner. Some of the little things we do can be disruptive and create unnecessary chaos and we often do them without thinking. For example, I don't favor discussing my relationship issues with my ex. Even though my ex knows me better than anyone and could probably provide better insight than any of my friends, our relationship is completely over and it's none of his business. I have over 600 contacts in my phone book full of personal friends and colleagues; there are plenty of shoulders to cry on if needed. On the flip side, I have had my business discussed with someone's ex. I didn't like it.

Contacting an ex and reminiscing about the past, seeking advice, or anything anyone else can do might be rocking the boat a little. Unless the information is relative to your ex, it can be disrespectful to the person you are with should you seek advice from them because you are turning to someone else when you need something, rather than the person you are in a relationship with. Most of the time one can find the information they need by using the internet!

Hidden Agendas

I've always had more male than female friends. The simple explanation for that is that I am a tomboy. By appearances, I am very feminine and though I have a nurturing instinct that often seems to be in overdrive, I am not a girlie girl. I'm not into fashion to the point of being accessorized to the gills before I walk out the door. My entire makeup collection would fit loosely inside a sandwich sized storage bag. I like racing cars and "fixing" things. Well, I'm not really into sports anymore, but I guess one could say I relate more to men, than I do to women.

That said, I am yet still a woman. During all my younger years it seemed as if my male friends genuinely liked me as a friend. They would say I was a "Guy with Tits" and they would invite me to do fun guy stuff. Most of the guys had girlfriends that I knew well and hardly any of them had any issues with me being around.

It isn't uncommon to have friends that are attracted to you. Sometimes the attraction is a mere and innocent crush and there is no intent on making something out of it, but as I have gotten older I have noticed how this has changed considerably. The boys that were always in the friend zone had started maturing and if they were single they would let their interests in me be known in what they thought were subtle ways.

Changes in behavior when others are around, particular gestures and body language are very telling signs someone wants to be more than friends. Being overly touchy feely when talking to you is a sign that someone is seeking physical affection. When I first moved to California I wanted to make new friends because I didn't know anyone. I would get invited to places by co-workers and I socialized online quite often. At one point I had made a good bit of new acquaintances both male and female. One particular person offered to show me around the city and keep me up to date on the hot spots, he seemed harmless. After our first few times hanging out he started placing his hand on my knee every time he would tell me something or if we were hiking and he wanted to show me something he would place his hand on the small of my back. It wasn't necessary to do either. If a situation presented itself and some sort of affectionate reassurance was warranted, it would have been nothing and as it turned out he indeed had become attracted to me during the course of our very short lived friendship. Or, maybe that could have been his motive all along?

There have been a few times during conversations discussing "singledom" that my friends have described their dream woman or ideal wife to be someone exactly like me and some have even said, "If we weren't friends, you would be the perfect one for me." This is a very awkward situation to be in. That statement was really bait being thrown out to see if I too were interested. I obviously wasn't and having to communicate this to a friend was more uncomfortable than a typical guy I'd gone out on a few dates with. There was always tension and a need to walk on eggshells when discussing my love life or theirs. Though I can't blame them for trying, because if I'd been interested what better person to be with than someone they knew they could trust and who knew them best? Unfortunately, the gamble altered our friendship forever.

On another occasion I had a friend who was always supportive of everything I did, but when it came to my romantic life he was a pure "Debbie Downer." It didn't matter how long I'd known someone before I began dating them or what they did for a living he would always say, "I hope you know what you're doing." He would often speak very poorly of them, even when it came to other men who were mutual friends he would always make sure I knew the dirt on them. I eventually got fed up and cut him loose after he crossed the line. I had planned a trip one weekend to the desert for some hiking and sight seeing with him and a mutual friend. At the last minute he was unable to go, but our mutual friend and I still kept our plans. Suddenly, he felt the need to divulge not so terrific details of our mutual friend's personal life. Presumably, because we were going to be alone together and this particular person was exceptionally attractive. If the information would have saved me from being murdered and buried in the desert it would have been necessary, but it was about a traffic infraction that happened 5 years previously. Aside from the pettiness of gossip, this behavior is also manipulative and a real friend wouldn't manipulate you.

From experience, I know when another woman is pursuing my man and is trying to become more than friends. My very first boyfriend was quite a handsome and a charming young man. Everywhere we would go girls would throw themselves at him, even with me being there. I would always feel disrespected, more so by him than the girls. He would never stand up and say they were being inappropriate. One day I became suspicious of a girl who hung around with some of the group of his friends. She was bringing him cookies and being over the top with her smiles. When I mentioned it to him of course he said it was all in my head. Later, after we split up he admitted that during our break up he and she engaged in a romance, in other words, they slept together. It wasn't all in my head, I was right.

A lot of my female friends had issues with women doing similar things. Some had situations in which a "friend" was buying clothes and home decor for their boyfriend when there was no special occasion that called for it. Boundaries were being overstepped and in the end it turned out the friend indeed was pursuing someone already taken.

I've had friends who would talk about other men in my life in front of a date. Not necessarily someone I was ever serious about, but just some someone from my past. It was always a strategy to turn off my date. This would happen with both male and female friends. The men sometimes had a crush on me and the women were so miserable in their own relationships they would try to sabotage mine to make themselves feel better. As juvenile and petty as it was, I actually used it to my advantage. It made it a lot easier to "thin the herd." I was able to deduce whether or not my date was jealous, insecure, or intelligent enough to see through what was going on.

Frenemies

Have you ever had a person you considered to be a friend, even though it seemed as if their life mission was to prove you wrong or to publicly humiliate you in some way? We all have them at some point in life. They hang out with us like friends, they keep in touch like friends, but they're not friends. They disguise themselves as someone with a sincere and invested interest in our lives while inside they despise everything about us. They challenge everything we do or say and they belittle or ridicule our relationships openly. Everything they do is a negative contribution to your life, but they say they're just trying to help.

The frenemy that stands out the most to me is someone I'd come to know for years. In the beginning she was intrigued by my complicated life story and she would often tell me how she would tell others about me as she found me fascinating. Later down the road she would be supportive of any of my romantic ventures and would say she was living life vicariously through me. As time went on she started becoming what I will refer to as a "contrarian." A contrarian is someone who regardless of what you say, they will argue the opposite. Everything was beginning to turn into a debate when we would talk.

One day, she came over to my house and went through my closet and criticized all my clothes and told me I needed a makeover. Things started to make sense; she had grown jealous of me.

Friends who witnessed some foul behavior at one of my birthday parties actually had warned me about her. Apparently, she was belittling me to some of my friends in a way that earned her the title, "Misses Bitter." I finally decided to sever ties once and for all when she began to play the antagonist on my social media wall. Whatever I would post, she would call into question my integrity, intelligence, and/or knowledge. One day, I decided to post the opposite of a previous post from weeks before and sure enough she fell for it. Just to argue, she debated her opinion as the exact opposite of what she had said before. At that moment it was clear she was just one who causes contention and quarrels, by definition, a makebate. She was offering nothing but discord for friendship and I simply deserved better. I completely severed all ties. I would later discover that she had a history of this behavior, which would explain why she didn't have many friends.

My environment was no longer one of chaos and I had many admirers who were sincerely fond of me as a human being. Being treated with kindness by people, who actually like you, makes it easier to differentiate a friend from a foe. Perhaps I allowed the situation play out a little too long, but live and learn.

Social Networking Troubles

The invention of social networking is what I call a double-edged sword. It is the most efficient resource to track down long lost friends and the easiest way to stay updated with the goings on amongst friends and family, I even located my siblings there. When it comes to finding people, it simply can't be beat. On the other hand, however, it also means that those characters that you'd rather not reconnect with have a way to track you down as well. Even if you set your privacy so that others cannot find you, just remember there is always 6 degrees of separation and where there's a will, there's a way.

On numerous occasions I have logged into my Facebook account and found a message or a friends request from the ex of a person I was presently dating. A message is usually something like a warning out of concern for my well-being or it's a congratulatory well-wish along the lines of, "I am so happy for you and _____. He deserves the best and I wish nothing but the best for you both." Both are absolutely unnecessary. Not knowing the ex or having any sort of exchange with them online made me question their motives. Think about it? What I discovered was malicious intent that was often followed by cyber-stalking.

I had a run in with one particular girl who had a long history of trying to befriend the girlfriends of someone who I was dating. All the girls she would contact thought the gesture was weird and everyone involved agreed it was suspect, but the girl did not find it a bit strange at all. One of the girls before me recalled her relentlessly sending a friends requests and would cancel to resend after each time it was rejected or ignored. Neither of us had met this girl before nor had we any sort of exchange with her so there was no reason to initiate a friendship. When she was confronted she said the reason she wanted to be friends was because she believed we all had some common interests. We had nothing in common whatsoever, the only thing we really had in common was a romantic history with the same man.

Another bizarre individual who lurked about in the cyber world was a woman who was not anyone's ex, but she was avidly trying to make her presence known. She had previously had an exchange with a guy I was dating before he and I had even met. She was an older lady who was also a self-proclaimed psychic. I had no idea who she was, but at one point she was posting nice comments on our photos, in return we had a bit of an exchange. She relocated all the way from the west coast to live in a small town in the mid-west to be near the guy after we split. They had never met. Through close friends I heard that they started a relationship of sorts and then split as he found her to be a little odd, okay, a lot odd. When she moved away from him wouldn't you know some of her friends were posting comments on my photos out of the blue? It was easy to put two and two together, so I just ignored them. Two years later, there she was again posting comments on how great I looked for my age and how my "positive" attitude is outstanding. Two years later and she is still obsessing.

Why can't we be Facebook friends?

I think it's fair when someone is reluctant to become Facebook friends with someone they're casually dating. Again, we share the most intimate details of our lives on Facebook when you think about it. Many of us have highly visible access to our closest friends and family, so it's wise to keep such things sacred from someone you hardly know.

However, when you've been dating a while and they still won't let you inside their Facebook world it may be a red flag. It often means there is someone around who doesn't need to see you. Your presence might make them become hurt or angry and as a result they might cause discord and drama in his or her life. As I've gotten older my online activity is less because I'm actually involved with being more productive outside the cyber world and if someone is involved to the extreme in which their life is consumed with it to where it might cause problems, I am less likely to pursue them anyway.

Now, I will say that I've dated guys before who'd remained Facebook friends with their exes and wouldn't add me simply because they didn't want them to know about me. This showed me that their ex still controlled them because they chose to appease someone from their past instead of considering the person present in their life. Obviously I felt is was disrespectful and that since they had no control over their decisions, but was rather letting their ex control them (still,) it was a sign of weakness which was very unattractive to me. Other times, they didn't want me to see someone...because they thought it might hurt my feelings...both scenarios meant "emotional baggage," which was something I have no interest in.

A few of my friends have said they didn't want to be friends with the person they were dating for fear of stumbling across something they didn't want to see and it would turn them off. If pessimism leads one to believe a person is the type who has something "bad" to see, then why are they even considering pursuing them in the first place? Unless they truly like disappointment to do so seems like a waste of time.

One scenario we seldom admit is that we are in fact the ones hiding something! If we are being completely honest about our relationship status and dating habits we should have nothing to hide. I tend to add everyone I date because if I think someone is really going to be a problem I'm just not going to deal with them in life much less Facebook. If something doesn't pan out I will either remain friends, or delete them if they annoy me. Most of the time when I sever our Facebook connection they don't even notice, but then sometimes I will get a text asking, "Why did you delete me?" I think if they can't figure it out or if they put that much value on being my Facebook buddy then I made the correct decision in letting them go.

Clueless

Are we clueless? I think many of us know when we are doing things we will later regret; our ego just won't let us admit it. We know when we are behaving in an undesirable way, but yet we continue. It may take some of us a little longer to process information, but I do not believe any of us are clueless.

When someone says they're not interested instead of accepting reality we believe we can change them or even manipulate them into falling in love with us.

How many times have we searched for answers online, bought books, or even attended seminars teaching us how to be what he or she wants?

Have you ever had your cards read or had a session with a psychic to see what is going on when you have felt a little uneasy about someone?

We do these things simply because we fear rejection. In the past when I was the recipient of rejection by someone I was fond of I would become frustrated and angry. How dare they reject me? I would become so consumed with finding the answer as to what it was about **them** that made me an undesirable mate. I would read books and search websites endlessly for the answers, searching for that perfect answer that would make me feel better about being dumped. Regardless the answer, all roads led back to me.

The obvious thing to do then would be to change myself to conform to what **they** wanted right? Wrong! A life full of games and pretending only leads to more break ups and heartaches.

We need others to back us up so we do not feel like complete idiots for wasting our time and we discuss any possibility he or she might be scared or unsure of how they feel, with anyone who will listen. I know I have been there. I've sat at a table with a tarot spread before me just so someone could tell me what I already knew, "You're feeling troubled about your love life and someone in it. Don't worry, you will see this person again." Did you know more women than men see psychics and most of the time a woman sees a psychic it's about love and it is most often about a breakup of sorts or finding Mr. Right?

I have over romanticized situations and been devastated when the romance fizzled. In desperate attempts to keep the fire burning at times I have lost my identity. For instance, I once dated a guy who was a big drinker. He always wanted to do happy hour or anything he could to get out of the house. Since I don't drink and I am very much a homebody, he did not feel we were a good match. I just could not accept it, even though it was the truth.

Although I did not start drinking, I forced myself to go out and do things I did not enjoy. I started going out more and being around people who were wasted. I told myself I was compromising, but all I was truly doing was denying that I was trying to change myself to be with this particular man.

Some relationships are like bad B movies, the cover looks amazing, the synopsis fascinates you, after a short while into it you find the story weak, riddled with contradictions and bad acting, you're tempted to leave but you give it a chance, you stay until the end, and then you realize you should have left a long time ago.

Many of us enter the search for Mr. or Mrs. Right with foolish optimism. We encounter those who have very few things we like about them, while everything else is just one big red flag after another. I wasn't colorblind and not seeing the red flags, I was just being self-destructive when I gave a chance to someone I knew was never going to work out before we'd even met.

Have you ever found yourself romantically involved with a mooch or a deadbeat? Well, I have several times, but the worst one was the last. In Los Angeles one might find themselves surrounded by millions of lost souls, the emotionally unavailable, the jaded, and pretentious people. Because of this, for some reason there is a longing for "Boys from the Mid-west." They are supposed to know how to treat women and be more grounded, not to mention they are said to be more masculine. This guy could not have proven that stereotype more wrong.

He hadn't had a steady job in 10 years and he had every excuse imaginable for not working. He claimed the government would take his wages because of unpaid student loans, in addition to fear of exacerbating a preexisting injury and he felt he had no experience for the jobs he was being offered. My first thought was, I am dating a lazy, self-defeating "man-child". I later tried to justify his behavior by trying to convince myself he just needed a little guidance because he was from a small town. That was just me being in denial, yet again. The truth is, there are hundreds of successful people in Los Angeles from even smaller towns.

His friends contacted me after I dumped him and said he'd been this way for the past ten years. Several of them told me he was "that guy" who conveniently leaves his wallet at home when the bill comes after a meal. Although he'd told me he was just visiting his parents he had actually been living with them for the past 3 years. I was embarrassed, but I was certainly never clueless. My gut told me he was bad news, but I kept trying to convince myself I was wrong for the sake of being in a relationship.

You have to let it go

I have been in some really horrendous relationships. Considering the risqué lifestyle I once led, what would one expect? I could write a book and preach forgiveness, but I am going to tell you the truth, my truth, about how important forgiveness is and how sometimes no forgiveness is necessary, you just simply let it go and move on.

In every relationship you have whether it's short lived or long lasting, you will always learn something. You may learn how to identify and empathize with others even after they have broken your heart. You may learn how to laugh when someone tries to play you, instead of plotting to get even. The lesson can be great or small in scale, but what you choose to do with what you've learned will play the biggest role in your life when it comes to romance and simple happiness.

What could be worse than someone breaking up with you via text message on the way to your dad's funeral? This most egregious act of uncouthness actually happened to me.

I was the purported girlfriend of an actor I'd met through a friend. Oddly, we discovered we'd both lived in Knoxville at the same time and though we ran in the same social circle, some how we'd never managed to meet. Perhaps that was for the best. As many actors do, he was going through a financial struggle and the acting thing just wasn't working out. It seemed his career as an actor had peaked some 10 years before when he was a reoccurring actor on a soap opera produced by the one and only, Aaron Spelling.

After I'd received the news that my father had passed away, my first instinct was to call the person closest to me, which was my boyfriend. He didn't answer so I left a detailed message on his voicemail and I'm certain there was a bit of sadness or distress in my tone. Hours went by and no word from him. I called him a few more times, but still no answer. I needed a ride to the airport and thankfully two of my friends were available to come to my aid. A few moments before they arrived at my house, he returned my call. He immediately started telling me about a part he landed that would be filmed in South Africa and how excited he was and all.

After about 15 minutes of his narcissistic rambling I interrupted him and said, *"Didn't you listen to my message? My dad died today."* His reply was, *"No. Sorry to hear that. Are you going home?"* after I told him when my flight was leaving, he resumed telling me about his movie. He didn't ask if I needed anything and he didn't even offer to give me a ride to the airport.

The following day after I'd been to the funeral home to view my dad's casket I was mortified. The reality had sunk in that my beloved father was no longer. I would never hear his voice again or hear him laugh and tell me how silly I was. I felt as if my heart had been ripped out of my chest and squeezed. I was at the worst point of the day, and then suddenly my phone rang. It was my boyfriend calling again. He was calling to say he was sorry for the way he acted and explained that he was just not good at handling "death." Wouldn't you know it, right after I let my guard down he tried to finish the story he was telling me about his upcoming trip to South Africa! I said, *"Are you kidding me?"* and I hung up. The next afternoon, I was on the way to the funeral home to bury my father and I got a text message from him that read:

> *"I can't be in a relationship right now. It's just not a good time for me. I don't want to have kids and I don't want to get married. Sorry."*

Months went by and I eventually forgave him, but I also forgot all about him. I talked to him a few times and he never brought up what happened, so I just moved on and far away leaving him no way to find me, or so I thought. Almost a year had gone by and he started calling and emailing me again, pretending he needed a contact for someone in the auto industry as he was in the market for a new car. I gave him the info and answered a couple of his questions and left it at that. Of course, his next question would be to know when we were going to go out. I immediately let him know it wasn't happening. I didn't hear from him again until he created a fake profile on MySpace to lure me out to meet him. He posed as an actor in need of headshots and since I was a known photographer in our circle he thought it would be a good ploy. After the third or so exchange with his character I knew it was him and I once again I shut him down, but this time I wasn't as friendly. I brought up the past and informed him of his narcissistic personality disorder and let him know that what he did was considered stalking and I would get a restraining order if he ever contacted me again. He did however contact me several months later through a mass email. It was a link to an article he was writing for a Texas based women's magazine, he was giving relationship advice. I didn't even bother to read it, but instead I buried my head in the sand.

I have learned a lot from my past relationships like how to forgive for the unspeakable and to recognize the signs that someone might have the potential to be someone I'm going to wish I'd never met. Unfortunately, there are a lot of bitter and angry people out there who have defined forgiveness as a sign of weakness in character and by doing so one becomes a victim or an enabler. However, when you forgive someone it doesn't mean you are weak or inviting them back into your life, for the very definition of forgive is to stop feeling angry or resentful toward (someone) for an offense, flaw, or mistake. You have simply chosen the path to a peaceful existence over one of grudges and unhappiness.

Though I have been in relationships with awfully deceptive men, I don't distrust every man I encounter merely because of his gender. I'm not a man hater and I believe both men and women contribute to their fair share of heartbreak and turmoil in their relationships. Many women do not see the irony of being a man-hater. How do they expect a man to fall in love with a woman who hates him? It would be like French kissing a shark.

A sign of a "hater" is someone who generalizes men and women. When they go on a bad date or encounter a situation in which the person opposite them behaves badly they chock it up to the gender and say things like, "Men are such assholes!" When really, only that particular person is whom they should be calling an asshole. In fact, all men and women are not bitches or assholes. I personally know a lot of outstanding and loving men and I'm pretty sure I am not often called a bitch. Maybe there is a reason those who generalize often find themselves lovelorn? Perhaps they are in denial or unaware of the vibe they send out into the universe where Mr. or Misses Right awaits them? I hear it from men all the time, "women are gold diggers, scandalous, or bitches." Usually, it comes from someone who has gotten burned by these types of women. Then they turn around and complain about quality women being in such short supply. A "quality" woman is usually attracted to a quality man and such a man would not place her into the group of bitches merely because of her gender. Such guys tell me I'm different right before they ask me out. I may be different, but I think their attitude needs some serious adjusting so I am never interested. I know better exists.

Should you have expectations from those you date or your relationships? Absolutely. Some argue not to have expectations. I don't see the logic in that. If people didn't have expectations then they would be dating aimlessly, I guess some like that though. When I date someone I expect them to treat me with kindness and respect our relationship. When they fail to do so I remove myself from the relationship. If a man portrays himself as a compassionate individual, I am going to expect him to treat others with kindness and if he doesn't I am going to question his character. If you communicated your expectations of marriage as the end result of your relationship, you may have expected a proposal by your 15th year together. When you are in a committed relationship, faithfulness of your partner is expected. I think people believe it makes them appear to be more grounded and like they are living in "the now" to say they have no expectations, when actually if one had no expectations then everything would be acceptable.

When I was younger I had a certain type, which was mainly the rocker type. Now, I date a variety of types of men. I date different races, different professions, and different social classes, so one cannot say I have one type. Some say when you have different types of people you are attracted to, it means you are desperate. I tend to look at it simply not being racist, materialistic, or superficial. To be clear, I am not saying that I don't have standards. When I am interested in someone and there is the smallest suspicion they're irresponsible with their livelihood, I won't bother getting to know them further.

I met a guy a few years ago at work; he was a well-mannered and poised man around 50 years old. Our initial conversations were mostly business related, but I was slowly getting to know him personally. After I left the company where we'd met, we started chatting more and had lunch a few times. A mutual attraction seemed to be blossoming, until I saw his living conditions. I am not referring to a dirty home or anything of that nature. He was living in a weekly rental efficiency hotel located in a sketchy part of town. He had 3 high-end vehicles parked outside, but wasn't able to afford an actual apartment or home? He told me that he had been renting a house and suddenly the owner kicked him out and left him nowhere to go. It had been over 2 months. Having struggled when I first moved to Los Angeles I knew it could be difficult to find a place you liked, but it's not that difficult for someone who has good credit, good rental history, and a couple months rent as a deposit if you don't! Someone who could afford such expensive cars should have the financial resources to downsize or simply relocate to another dwelling at around the same cost. Something did not quite make sense. Later, we had dinner and our conversations revolved around his need for money and desire to reinvent himself. When he started making references implying that I was "his woman" I knew, he wasn't for me.

Another guy I met for only one date was someone who got too caught up in the Hollywood nightlife and spent all his money on parties and material items to impress the superficial people whom he didn't know. He didn't have a car anymore and he was behind several months on his rent. He started telling me what a great poker player he was and that if I had any money I should give it to him and he could double it for me. Of course after I said "no" he wasn't interested in me anymore.

Having stability can make one more a target for parasites. I've started recognizing constant complaints about financial burdens as a sign of parasitical behavior or someone looking for help out of a situation. Freeloaders often drop hints about needing a place to crash or they ask if you know of any ways they can make a fast buck because they are in desperate need of money. What they are doing is playing upon your emotions hoping you will pity them enough to take them in. In most cases when someone is truly in a dire situation and isn't looking for someone to take advantage of, dating is their last priority.

> *Some relationships are like having ice cream when you're lactose intolerant, even though it's wonderful while you're having it; you know you're going to pay for it later.*

Mute

When my television is turned up, but I suddenly need a little silence I often press the button that says, "mute." There have been many times I've wished I could have used this feature on some of the men I've dated. Men tend to be somewhat less emotional than women, but there are a few exceptions.

"I was like, mute."

I said, as I described the outcome of a quarrel with an ex to my best friend.

Some men like to nag about the same things women are known to nag about: their face being bloated, lack of attention making them feel neglected, the attention given not presented in the way they like, and so on, and so on... MUTE

I reconnected with an old flame from fifteen years ago. We had an off again, on again relationship for a few years when he was at the peak of his professional career, but we split up when I started to mature and realize how bad his attitude was and he became less appealing.

Thinking he may have also grown up and changed, I agreed to meet to see if there was any fire to rekindle. When he picked me up at the airport he had not aged a bit and was actually quite more handsome than when we dated.

Things went okay the first night; however the next day I was quickly shown he hadn't changed at all, he was still a misogynistic control freak. While on our way to breakfast one morning I was a little cold so I turned on the heated seat I was sitting in. He leaned over and turned it off and then scolded me like a child for turning it on without asking him. The rest of the time I was there I stayed in my room to avoid his relentless need to argue and his negative energy. I left the next day and never contacted him again.

I believe I have changed for the better and by knowing this I must apply the same logic to others. I gave my ex the benefit of the doubt, but he once again confirmed I deserve better than him. At my worst stage in life, he wasn't for me and now at my best he definitely isn't. I believe it's worth the opportunity to find out if someone you loved before could relight your fire, as long as you don't put any more energy into it when there's just nothing there. The past is supposed to be a learning experience, let it teach you and keep moving forward with what you've learned.

My Random Little Survey Said...

Just for fun I conducted a random survey and it became obvious how skewed the perception of men and women is towards each other. It became pretty apparent that perhaps we are being misled by others and are allowing their words to dictate the way we behave. There are a lot of double standards and we over complicate things.

One-Night Stands

To hear my gal pals tell it, they've never had a one night stand because it's whorish; however, according to my survey, more women had one night stands and have also used someone for sex than will admit. Because many believe it to be "whorish," they are reluctant to admit to this because it may taint their respectable image, thus ruin their chances of "being found" because it makes them less than the perfect woman.

One-night stands are when you meet someone and have sex and never see him or her again. I've had my share of one-night stands and though I can only speculate why someone else might be so reckless with their sex life, I can certainly tell you why I was. I was willing to simply give myself away because I didn't care about my welfare, nor did I have concern for any of the risks involved with my behavior. I had an extremely low sense of self-worth and there was usually a lot of drugs and alcohol involved. It's easier not to feel shame for something you can't remember doing.

Though a lot of men are under the delusion that sleeping with a lot of random women and being reckless makes him some sort of a rock star, I tend to think he must feel the same way about himself as I did, feeling like anything is good enough and not having any standards. Because of my past I am able to exercise a little bit of empathy toward men that behave this way because I can relate to them. However, I'm in a place in life now where I can't find myself being attracted to any man who doesn't love and respect himself enough to hold his body sacred.

The Alpha Male

Most women didn't like men who were macho or machismo. Contrary to what many think, the pompous and arrogantly broadcasted alpha male behavior is considered embarrassing, annoying, and rude. Sometimes men will refer to themselves as an alpha male, when they're really just a contemptibly obnoxious person, or a "jerk" if you will.

To some, a jerk can be someone who doesn't hold the door for a woman or someone who shows extreme inconsideration to others. For example, I knew someone who would take a larger portion of food leaving none to be divided equally between others and sometimes they would eat all of something without offering any. Sometimes these are just things people do that haven't learned proper etiquette and good manners. I hold the door for anyone walking behind me regardless of his or her gender and if it comes down to the last bit of food at the dinner table, I will offer it even if I want it for myself.

A "jerk" is the guy who thrives on the attention he receives by using shock factor; they say and do things in a way to intentionally provoke a negative reaction. For example, if a guy tells me I have "nice tits" or a "nice ass," they think they're being funny by being lewd. I see them as the belligerent drunk on the mechanical bull. He climbs aboard as the audience cheers, recognizing him as the guy who seems to be braver than all the other drunk guys and it didn't matter whether or not he fell off, he received some sort of attention... attention that he sought to give his insecurity a boost for a short lived moment that will fade as soon as either the booze wears off or when the spectators turn their attention elsewhere. Fairly confident that I have a sense of humor I can assure you my lack of attraction to obnoxious and pompous men is that I simply think their brain cells function differently than that of what I consider to be **my** kind of man.

I've had men tell me that they see I'm an "alpha" and they are also an alpha. I think any man who announces he is an alpha male usually isn't, nor does he try really hard to be, because if he were truly an alpha he would not have to.

Mean Girls

Of the men who took the survey, a majority said they did not like 'bitches' or unkind women. So for those of you women following that belief that if you play hard to get or play mind games to intentionally mess with a man's emotions, think again. Additionally, when I asked those men why so many men date "bitches" if they are so undesirable, they said it is because the men who tolerate poor and abusive behavior are doormats. Why would you want to walk all over someone? And, why would you want to be with a man who would allow it?

Money

Most women believe when a man spends an excessive amount of money before getting to know her it meant he must really like her, while fewer believed he's just being showy. I think the latter, after all, how can he know if he likes her that much, if he hardly knows her?

The men said they do it because they're trying to impress the woman with their money. If a man drops a ton of cash on a woman for material things without making her "earn" it they believe her company can be bought or that she is materialistic. A nice an accepted gesture to show sincere interest is a simple bouquet of flowers, unless she really is materialistic then she will move on to someone who will buy her more glittery things. It all depends on what the man thinks of himself and what kind of woman he really wants.

Approach

Most men said they would never approach a woman because they fear rejection or they think the woman is already taken, but the women said they actually would speak to a man if he simply approached them by asking for their name! It's really all in the approach for me. I won't engage with a man who is aggressive in his approach. For example, when I lived in Atlanta, guys would physically grab my arm and pull me over to them when I was walking by to ask my name. To be frank, I would be uneasy if a random guy walked up to me and said, "What's your name?" even if he were polite. It would work better for me if he introduced himself first and then asked my name. Regardless of approach, if he is not my type the end result will be the same, meaning there will be no connection. If he is my type and approaches me the aggressively, then he's already taken himself out of the running.

Sexual Innuendos

When it came to sexual references, many women felt if a man mentioned sex in conversation jokingly or not before or on the first date it was disrespectful. I was once on the telephone with a guy after just arranging a date and he felt he needed to tell me that the last girl he'd dated sent him a photo of her breasts via text when he was at dinner with his kids earlier. He also stated that being a man, of course he looked. I didn't even have to think twice and cancelled our date. Another time sex was mentioned was when I was actually on a "pre-date" for coffee with a different guy. We'd been talking for a while, but not near long enough for him to have felt comfortable telling me that he was eight years old the first time he saw a woman's vagina, but he referred to it as a "pussy." I felt it was lewd and pretty much told him to lose my number.

When a guy mentions sex on the first date I will change the subject and never go on a second date. Every single time I've given a guy a chance that mentioned sex, even in a joke, he turned out to be a real sleaze. Mentioning sex on the first date was a way to probe to see what kind of date I was going to be. When I laughed, it showed interest, when I commented, it showed interest, and at the end of the date they were putting their hands where they shouldn't or inviting themselves to my home. While I thought I was being polite in an awkward conversation, they were receiving mixed signals.

A lot of guys will admit to talking about sex with women they hardly know, but are trying to get to know. Some say they feel comfortable with the woman so they thought they could talk about anything. While the majority of them said it was because they want to get a reaction so they could see how far she was willing to go.

Chapter III

Start Dating Better

Details

What's the point of dating? Some like to date casually just to have something to do to fill a void, while others do it in search of a lifelong commitment. It's important to know major details in the beginning. Minor details can be resolved by working together or simply ignoring them. For example, if a man leaves the toilet seat up, is it really the end of the world? Does he snore? Does he leave a mess everywhere he goes? Are any of these things really a deal breaker when he has all the other qualities we look for? One topic that I find most important, which needs to be known before even going on a date is having kids. Of course you will most likely scare off any man if you start talking about having *their* child right off the bat. However, if you want kids and he doesn't then you really shouldn't waste any time getting to know each other. Children are a very important part of life and to some being a parent is what they believe will complete them.

I am leaving my child bearing years, though with the help of new technology I am sure I could stretch them out if I wanted to. If I wanted to, however, I do not. At times my choice not to bear children offends people. They often assume my decision is based on vanity, me not wanting to gain weight or get stretch marks, because we all know there are no skinny mothers in Hollywood. Or they assume that I don't like kids, which couldn't be farther from the truth. What they fail to realize is that I didn't say I didn't want kids, I said I didn't want to bear children. There are over 450,000 children in foster care in the United States, one of these days I would like to be a foster parent and perhaps adopt a child. I realize my view of what it is to be a parent may clash with others, that's why I believe it's important to let it be known upfront. Saying, "I want kids" to someone who wants to have his own kids may mislead him into believing there might be an opportunity to have them with me.

The subject of children should never be taken lightly. Many say they want children, but when it comes down to planning parenthood, they realize providing for a child financially and emotionally is not for them and they back out. Women and men will say what they think the other wants to hear when it comes to having a family simply to get the dating process started. It's happened to me on several occasions. I'd made my stance clear, leaving nothing to be misinterpreted and at some point either someone wanted to have kids of their own, or didn't want kids at all, not even adopted or fostered.

In the past I've dated men who had children and often found myself attached to the child or being in the middle of arguments between them and the child's mother. With some, the mother would use the child as a way to throw a monkey wrench into our plans by suddenly dropping them off without notice or threatening to deny visitation if the father didn't comply with her needs.

Don't lie about your kids!

I think one of the worse things anyone could ever do is lie about their child. It is the ultimate, undeserved insult for a child to be unclaimed like baggage. My mother kept my existence a secret from many people; such news was much easier for me to process than I could have imagined it would have been if I were a child.

What on earth would make someone deny they have a child? Usually, if the person is not present in the child's life it's easy to deny the child exists, but if he or she is present and doesn't want anyone to know, it's often because of the risk of damaging his or her image. For example, I dated a guy once who shamelessly lied about being the father of one of his children. He had three children, 2 were black and 1 was mixed with Caucasian, guess which one he didn't claim? There were photos throughout his house of the child but he claimed it was his niece. A mutual friend of mine told me he knew the child's mother. It made no sense, why would he say the child was his niece? It had to be his niece; after all, he had 2 other children with two other women, which he proudly claimed, so why would this third little one be any different? One day, one of his other children referred to the little girl as his little sister and the truth finally came out. He never said why he didn't claim the little girl, but it didn't matter. I had never been exposed to a lie of this degree so it was very unsettling and I later found this man had some more complicated and serious flaws in his character. He was a pathological liar and an emotionally and physically abusive narcissist.

How to meet people

ONLINE DATING

There are hundreds of different ways to meet people, but if you don't have a lot of free time for in-person socializing online dating is a great option. I have been using this method since it first launched in the late 90's. There has been a negative stigma attached to it for the longest time, but in fact it is no different from going to the gym or a bar to meet people. You will come across the same issues and annoyances as you will anywhere and those you find in the other places are using online dating to meet people as well.

Much like a gym or bar, one can find men who are seeking a quick hook-up while they deceive the women by promising them the moon and the stars, but unlike a gym or bar, there are men searching for a long time commitment, and possibly their first, second, or third wives. The same applies to women, there are women seeking a sugar daddy pretending to want love when all they really want is financial support, and then there are women looking for a loving husband. Making a connection with someone you meet online is not a myth, I have many personal friends who have met their spouses online and are currently still married.

There are a lot of free dating sites these days offering the same results as paid sites. All dating sites have the same typical absurdities though; men who copy and paste their introduction email and never read your profile. Many believe it is a numbers game and will mass email everyone they find attractive.

Paid sites can run from $29 to $59 per month, but because many have the same members I always sign up for the free trial. I paid for a membership several years ago, but got a full refund because they could not find a match for me. The site turned out to be Christian based and because I'm not religious I didn't list a religion and it was making me incompatible with their members.

I signed up again several years later and yielded only five compatible results. All five matches lived more than 20 miles from me and in Los Angeles that's at least an hour drive. Interesting enough, this particular site claimed to have hundreds of thousands of members within my area but all they could match me with were five people.

Additionally, when setting up my profile there was no option for mixed race, or selecting two races. When I selected the second choice, the first choice would deselect. Selecting only one would be misleading and untrue and in this day and age there are a lot of mixed raced people so it should be an option. For me, the only good thing about this site was the mandatory personality questionnaire, which gave an accurate account of how I saw myself.

The Profile

Many will practically post their resume, or a condensed autobiography, in the "about me" portion of their profile, most of the time it tells nothing of their true personality. For me, there does not need to be more than a paragraph or two to draw my attention as long as it's interesting. It is apparent the icebreaker is very difficult for many to devise, so there should be enough, but not too much, to get the conversation started, too much information leaves no questions to be asked or comments to be made.

Sometimes the "about me," starts with a line that says they're too good for online dating and are embarrassed to resort to such desperate measures. Starting off with something negative will set the tone for the rest of the content. For me it's a put down for everyone online, including me.

Almost every profile says he or she is "easy going with a great outlook on life." If this is the case why are so many looking for Mister and Misses Right? They should be around every corner.

One has to be realistic. A profile with a balance of good and bad shows he or she can recognize pain and happiness. I am more likely to engage with someone who has some sort of "realness" in their profile, sometimes their realness might not be what I am looking for, but knowing up front cuts down on wasted time and being disappointed later.

Those who have only good things to say about themselves I am the most leery of. Often I have engaged with those who portrayed themselves as having the temperament of The Dalai Lama, however, they were quite the opposite once I got to know them better.

I was chatting with this young man a few years ago on Match.com. He was really sweet, but the longer we talked he began to unload his troubles and heartaches. I asked if he was sure he was ready to pursue dating or if he would like to have a friend, he took it the wrong way and immediately became defensive. He lashed back and said, *"You're not all that, and don't forget you're 34 and on Match.com honey."* I was shocked because his profile read all good things, had it been mixed with some sense of irritability, I would have known how to better approach him, or at least would have been prepared for his harsh and petty remarks.

A profile with mostly rants of negative sarcasm is usually never a mirage for something pleasant. In many cases people project the way they feel about themselves, therefore, a profile with all negativity often means the person has a negative outlook. Some are not happy and cannot communicate with others unless they're complaining or being antagonistic. That doesn't work for me. I just keep scrolling, because there is nothing I can contribute and I am certainly not the person who is entitled to write this person and tell him how to change his life to be more appealing by my standards. So many people do it though.

A man approached me once in his early 50s who said he liked the things I said in my profile and though he didn't feel we had anything in common romantically it would be nice to be acquainted and perhaps we could be friends. His profile had quite a bit of negativity but since I had no interest in dating, I accepted his friend's request. I thought it would be okay since my personal information couldn't be viewed and some of my closest male friends were men I met off dating sites. Unfortunately, he turned out to be one of those people who used Google all day to search for the latest racist and political news to post.

He seldom had any updates unless they were inflammatory propaganda about politics and religion, or negative status updates. It became clear he was a bigoted racist, so after only a few weeks I decided to sever contact, as we clearly were not like-minded.

Creating a profile

Creating a dynamic profile all depends on what you are looking for. I recently had a man approach me for advice on how to stop attracting what he referred to as, "Ugly women and gold diggers." When I asked for his definition of ugly, he went on with a story about how some women are ugly on the outside and beautiful on the inside, but he just cannot get past their ugliness. I found this guy to be physically attractive until I read what he had to say. It makes me cringe when I hear someone use the word "ugly" to describe someone's physical appearance. I tend to believe they are projecting how they feel about their own self-image. Who are they to determine what is "ugly?" As they say, beauty is in the eye of the beholder. Why couldn't he simply say there were women he wasn't physically attracted to personally?

Shallowness will always dissolve any good impressions I have of anyone. Nonetheless, when I viewed his profile his income was listed at over $100,000 and he had photos of his car, which happened to be a high-end luxury vehicle. He had all the right bait to attract one of the things he claimed to want to avoid, gold diggers. This young man appeared to have a below average level of common sense.

Misrepresentation of physical appearance is the biggest complaint with online dating. One person will demand everyone use a recent and clear photograph, while at the same time he or she is using a photo that is old, enhanced or in some cases, diffused. Both men and women are looking for perfection, when in fact they are far from perfection themselves. They focus on the profile that meets a majority of their checklist requirements without much regard to what the person has written about himself or herself. Is he between the ages of 40-50? Yes (✔). Does he want kids? Yes (✔). Is he employed? Yes (✔). He has all those things, but has nothing in common with you and in some cases his checklist is inaccurate.

But even when they're being truthful about the superficial things on their profile, their truth can be a turn off. What people disclose about themselves in their "basic list" can be a really good way to judge their character without having to even read the first paragraph of their profile.

Income

Men who list their incomes are usually stretching it a bit, so it means they're lying, which speaks for itself. However, there are occasions when they are telling the truth. Some say they do it because they want to disclose everything about themselves so the woman will know she is entering a relationship with someone who is financially responsible. Again, we're talking about the profile, not the first few dates and is there really a time when you're in the beginning stages of getting to know someone that finances should be discussed?

I have dated millionaires who were financially irresponsible and had to get roommates to supplement their income in order to meet their monthly expenses, while I have dated men who made much less than a six-figure income, but never struggled financially because they lived within their means. Unless they're celebrities and their net-worth is broadcasted online, most people with millions or more down play their wealth, it's like being from old money. The amount of money one makes is irrelevant; it is how responsible they are with it that matters to me.

Photos

At a certain age, men with shirtless photos become more the butt of a joke than the object of my desire. I tend to question whether it's confidence or insecurity that makes a guy post photos without a shirt on, but I lean more towards insecurity. I can usually tell if a man is in shape by the way his clothes fit. When most men do what is needed to have a sculpted physique they usually have clothing to accentuate it as well. After all, it's not like he can enter places of business without wearing a shirt, so a topless photo is not necessary. Not only that, now everyone who uses online dating will know how he looks without a shirt, including all my friends, or other women I know.

"I have sexy photos up because they get me a lot of compliments." To me, this is a sign of a man who needs to be validated, because he is insecure about his looks.

If I see a photo of someone doing something silly in their 20's that children do, like teetering back and forth on a rocking horse or distorting their faces while sniffing an armpit, I might think it's funny or shows a sense of humor; but when I see recent photos doing the same exact things and he's well into his 40's, it's obvious that he hasn't matured very much or maybe he has Peter Pan Syndrome.

Peter Pan Syndrome-a male who has physically grown as an adult, but hangs on to his childhood to avoid assuming responsibility like a mature person.

Old photos

Digital cameras have been out for years and today's cell phones come standard with one, therefore, there is no excuse for not having a recent photo. It's really not a mystery, the main reason many use older photos is because they looked better then, than they do now.

How to dissect an email

My profile always had conversation starters like references to Eckhart Tolle, Criminology, and NASA. I don't think I could have made it easier with so many deliberate icebreakers, so when I got emails that said, *"Hi. I like your profile and would like to get to know you better,"* I never responded. If I had, I would have never gone on any dates due to being so tied up responding since that's what every other email said.

I often respond to those who make the effort even if I'm not interested. I think it's polite and I'm always open to making new acquaintances, however, it can be a slippery slope as you might be creating false hope of a romance.

If a guy only references my appearance with a comment like, *"You're hot,"* I won't engage. I'm not in my 20's anymore and most of the men who contact me aren't either, so even though I know it's meant to be a compliment, it just doesn't do anything for me. It's a vapid comment.

The Copy and Paster

One of the things people do is copy and paste their introductions. The intelligent and not so desperate are able to see how transparent this behavior is, but that doesn't stop people from doing it.

True Story

The same guy over a course of four years sent me the same exact email, which said, *"Where can a guy get to know a girl like you? The standard Starbucks meeting or Club Sushi?"* Not only that, he had used the same photo and he kept his age set at 34. He looked okay in his photo, but his profile looked to be a 4000-word rant without any breaks in between paragraphs. It looked as if he were online because he desperately needed to vent and was searching for someone who would listen.

After taking a year off from online dating, he found me again and sent email and used the exact same line; this time, I felt compelled to write back this time.

Since childhood, I have had an uncanny ability to remember details (when sober) of events and images; some say I am eidetic. For this, I was able to tell him how many times he sent the same email, his age had been listed as 34 years old for several years, and he had used the same photograph as well. He replied and said, *"Women don't respond most of the time when I make the effort so I don't bother."* His ideology was similar to those who made plans on how to spin their lottery winnings without actually buying a ticket. He thought he was so fantastic that he wouldn't have to put any effort toward making a connection and even after his way of doing things failed, he continued to do so.

In his mind, however, he believed he had made an impression since I could remember how many times he contacted me. He was right, but many things often leave lasting impressions, but some impressions are not always good.

Insanity: doing the same thing over and
over again and expecting different results.
-Albert Einstein

As entertaining as online dating can be with innocent absurdities, there are times you may come across a few creepy individuals. Be extra cautious of the ones who become possessive of you online. I would get over 100 emails per day. Unlike some, I didn't have time to read every email as soon as it hit my inbox. With some guys, I wouldn't even have a chance to respond before they would have sent me another email telling me off and calling me all sorts of names for not responding in a timely manner. At first I was annoyed by their behavior, but then I realized I had actually averted an undesirable situation. If someone is questioning or demanding of your time without even dating you, it's a huge red flag. Those are signs of controlling and obsessive behavior and in your future might be a very grim and potentially dangerous relationship.

I try to get a little more insight by asking a few simple questions. Some might call it a way to thin the herd. I list three simple questions to be answered in the beginning of my profile. When a man does not answer it means he did not read my profile, when he refuses to answer it means he's already disregarding me by being dismissive. I had one guy actually write me and tell me he wasn't going to answer my questions because he believed we should get to know each other his way. I politely wrote him back and said I wasn't interested because he'd already shown me that he could easily dismiss me and I was looking for a give and take relationship.

3 simple questions

I already know myself well enough to know what my quirks and pet peeves are as well as what works for me and what doesn't. The kind of questions I ask are the ones there can be no "right answer" for. If I were to ask someone if they wanted world peace, of course they would say yes. My goal was to get their opinion to gauge compatibility.

Here is a sample of my 3 questions:

How do you feel right now?

Again, this isn't a trick question and there is no wrong answer. It's just nice to know what kind of outlook on life someone has. Some people are downers, some are upbeat, and some see gloom and doom.

How do you feel about reality shows that showcase celebrities with volatile behavior?

This question might seem a bit silly, but I ask it with good reason. I have an immense dislike for reality shows in which people are made celebrities for wearing high fashion and being catty. I am confident I would not have much in common with someone who would find such things entertaining and I am certain I would not enjoy watching these shows with them.

Do you like cats?

It's really simple. I have cats, so if someone "hates" cats, there is no point to engage. If someone is more a dog person than a cat person it's alright, but I've actually had responses, "I hate cats." Hate is such a strong word and very telling of ones character who uses it.

Sometimes someone will answer with what I find to be acceptable for potential, but it doesn't automatically make them a match for me. At times there is no chemistry, so I won't pursue getting to know them romantically, but I am always open to being acquaintances.

Stop talking & meet, or stop talking and hang up.

There have been times when I've opened an introductory email with an enclosed telephone number. Even though today with things like Google Voice, which will forward calls to your telephone without having to jeopardize your privacy, it has been going on for years. I think it shows a sign of desperation and foolishness. After all, how does he know my profile isn't a fake? How does he know I'm not part of some internet scam? I also tend to think he's given his number out to all the other women he's contacted. I've recently discovered that sometimes it's someone committing identity theft as a prank by creating a fake profile and giving out the number so the person will intentionally be harassed. Because of both scenarios, I just skip to the next email without entertaining the idea of actually connecting.

I will usually engage in several email conversations before I agree to speak on the phone, I have to be comfortable first. Some guys want to talk on the phone right away to see if there is chemistry without having built up to a reason to find out. I've also had guys insist on calling me, but wouldn't exchange their numbers for mine and it was a red flag. There is always a reason they don't want **you** to call **them** and it's never a good one.

There are no rules for length of time you should talk on the phone before you meet; some like to meet right away while others like to take their time. You simply meet when you feel ready. However, I have learned the hard way that it is best to talk a bit before you decide to meet.

I have agreed to meet someone early on in the conversation, but by the end of the call they have said something that turned me off or made me decide they wouldn't be well suited for me. It is always awkward breaking a date because you have lost interest. It's better to be turned off on the phone rather than after you've met in person.

Having to sit through 15 minutes or longer of fighting being uncomfortable is exhausting. You will get to the point that you can't even look them in the face when you're talking.

There are so many people online; some are not as they portray themselves to be, while others are exactly what you see. I strongly advise trusting your gut instincts when it comes to meeting people. Be smart when it comes to you. Giving out your personal information like your full name so people can "Google" you is really naive. You are putting everything you love at risk when you give your information out to a complete stranger.

VOLUNTEERING AND EXPLORING GROUP INTERESTS

Aside from online dating, there are other ways to meet like-minded individuals. I'm not pushing people to volunteer so you can meet available singles. I run a soup kitchen in West Hollywood one day a week. Most of my team are actors, quite charming and handsome ones at that. After reaching out for others to volunteer by promoting what we do with photographs of our team, I had a lot of single women wanting to come down to volunteer, but their main goal was to meet the actors. That's going about it the wrong way. Someone who is pretending will not impress someone who does what we do because we pour our hearts into it. If you take one of your own interests and find an organization or a group who need help you can volunteer and make friends or at the very least be able to engage with like minds. For me, because of what I do within my organization people are always trying to introduce me to "fantastic single men" all the time.

When you volunteer, not only will you be helping your cause you may also tap in to a part of your soul that needs some healing. I've volunteered for the homeless throughout life, but my life changing moment was when I started with the Las Florists fundraiser. Las

Floristas was holding their annual headdress ball at The Beverly Hills Hotel and I was hired on as their event photographer. I had only researched the history of the event without digging into how the proceeds are distributed. When I arrived I was taken away by the "who's who" of Hollywood and the glamour and glitz of the venue. Some of the most affluent families where in attendance, all dressed to the nines, but there were others who impacted me more, in a different way. Off to the sides there were several children and adults in wheelchairs. Some of them were without any chance of being able to walk again, but they appeared so happy and hopeful and more importantly full of love. As I watched their smiling faces light up when people gathered around them I began to realize how precious life was. It was at that moment that I could feel my heart beginning to open up.

Once I viewed life from another perspective I began to realize all the things I complained about were not "real" problems. Not only that, gratitude that came from those I helped filled the void in my life. I was redirecting the energy from the men I dated, to those truly in need of help and for once I was being appreciated and the love was being reciprocated.

I'm not saying this is what you should do to meet people, but you have nothing to lose when it is something you are already interested in or if you are there for the greater good.

Interracial Dating

Interracial dating is so taboo in some areas of the United States, especially in the areas where I grew up. When I lived in Atlanta I had white girlfriends who only dated black men, while I had others who harbored obvious hatred towards them. I respect the practice of other cultures and the choice of others to stay within their race as long as their rules are not imposed on me. However, throughout life I have been bombarded with Non-Asian men who only dated Asian women. Apparently, some men prefer "my kind" because of many Asian stereotypes. We are supposedly docile and subservient. Sometimes random men will walk up to me and ask if I'm Filipino. No hello or nice day, just feel like knowing the ethnicity of a complete stranger will some how enhance their lives. I just say, "No," and keep moving most of the time.

I've actually had a DNA test that confirmed my ancestry; believe it or not I'm mostly Russian. More than half of my DNA descends from the Russian Far East. I liked the mystery of not knowing, but now that I do, it's much easier to explain. I can give a definitive answer and now all the unsolicited speculation is needless.

While I'm only a small percentage, Black New Guinean, some men seem to be infatuated with my "blackness." I dated a guy whom I truly thought had potential. He treated me well, I felt like we had a lot in common, and he had a positive attitude in the beginning, but when he discovered I was from Atlanta and a little black, he suddenly changed his attitude... and his vocabulary. He started walking around with his pants hanging off his butt and was constantly protesting all that was white. He went from saying things like, *That was an exquisite dessert by the chocolatier* " to saying like, *"You better git widdit. Ya heard!"* He associated my blackness to yet another typical black stereotype, speaking slang and being angry. After he purchased a fake "gold grill" (teeth caps made of gold) I'd decided I'd seen all I needed to see and just faded out. I think he knew why.

I've always dated men outside my race and never had a problem dating other races, but yet I have never dated an Asian. There weren't but a handful of Asians were I grew up and even though there are a lot here in Los Angeles, they just don't seem to go for me. I asked one of my Asian friends to shed some light on the subject and according to him, most Asian men who date within their race prefer their women to be docile and meek or at least have some Asian cultural upbringing. That was easy to clear up, as I am quite the opposite.   Then when it comes to Asian American men, they seem to prefer women outside of their race. Me with an Asian man seemed to be a battle I could never win.

Dating games

I never engage in dating games. I have no respect for anyone who does and when men try to "run their game" on me I see through it immediately and I handle it accordingly.

- Wait 3 days to call- I don't count the days, hours, or minutes with anyone so I wouldn't know if it had been three days or one week. I will probably shoot a text and invite him to accompany me to something I am **already** doing. I won't wait for him to contact me first, nor will I make up a reason to contact him. However, if I don't hear from someone after what I think was a nice time, I just figure he's not interested and move on. Not hearing from someone doesn't eat me up with curiosity anymore. It could be that I'm older or that I actually have other things to do that prevent me from pining away for someone I hardly know; or maybe it's because my life has changed in a way that I find it easier to attract men and I don't have to wait on anyone?

- Be intentionally unavailable or dismissive to make someone chase me is rude and not very becoming of an adult; it's also a waste of time. Sadly, I find it even hard to have respect for men who fall for these games. Chasing after someone who treats them poorly shows that he doesn't have self-respect for tolerating such behavior.

Many women feel accomplished and superior because they've hooked someone by using these tactics, but I think their behavior shows how desperate they are. They have a distorted view of themselves. They see themselves as conquers, but they are completely oblivious to the fact that they have had to result to such tactics because they are lacking what is desired to lure or capture the interest of someone naturally. I feel it is foul to treat people poorly in general, why would I reserve it for someone I felt was worthy of my time? It is hypocritical to demand to be treated with kindness and respect if we don't reciprocate.

Games can also backfire. The fear of rejection is what keeps us from showing our true feelings towards someone we admire. So we engage in "the games" to test the waters without realizing we could be potentially pushing the right person away. If you like someone you can let him or her know without awkwardness. When you are fond of someone you're dating and the feeling is mutual, length of time known and whether or not they're judging you for your feelings towards them just won't matter because you can't get enough of each other.

Chapter IV

Real Date Stories

Every time I would discuss the aftermath of a bad date my friends would tell me I could write a book on them. Instead of writing a book I thought I would just share a few of the worst stories here.

Check Please!

I met a guy out for a first date hike one day, it was a casual hike and just something to do that was different than the usual dinner and a movie. After the hike we decided to grab lunch at a nearby cafe. That's when I really got to know him.

During the conversation we got on the topic of various herbal cleanses and fasting. He mentioned a H2O fast he had done which helped him lose 50 pounds. Intrigued I wanted to hear more. Though I wanted to hear more about the cleanse itself, what I got was a bit of TMI. He told me he'd been coming off the cleanse for about a day and though he hadn't consumed any food the entire time, he felt like he needed to "use the bathroom." I thought he was going to leave it at that, but no, he proceeded.

"It was like a euphoric bowel movement, but it smelled worse than any I've ever had, it wasn't like the regular smell, and the stench was in the walls for 3 days. We had an earthquake that was about a 4 during the time I was in the middle of using the bathroom, if you know what I mean. The jolt from the quake knocked me off the toilet so you can imagine what I had to clean up. It took weeks to get the smell completely out of the house"

No matter how comfortable someone makes you feel, bowel movements should never be discussed during a meal, ever.

That's just gross!

Sometimes an uneventful date can be a breath of fresh air, until they pull off a shoe and take a whiff...

I went on a date with a guy who I'd been introduced to through a co-worker; he was the average, corporate executive with an office in one of Los Angeles's famous skyscrapers. Our first date was nice and quiet, just a simple dinner date. He was kind of boring, but I liked that about him. Since there were no obvious red flags, he peeked my interest for a second date. Our second date was the same, nothing spectacular, no bells, or whistles. All seemed to be going well.

When we arrived back to his place he offered to give me a tour of his house. It was a beautifully remodeled cottage. It was warm and inviting and exceptionally clean. He offered me water so I took a seat on the couch with him. We chatted a bit and I was still enjoying myself. I was comfortable. When out of nowhere he started complaining about a foul smell and discovered it was himself.

"Wow my shoes stink," he said as he lifted his foot to his nose and took a whiff. After a brief moment of confusion, he took off his sock and lifted his pale and sweaty foot to his nose. *"It's not my shoes that stink, it's my feet!"*

The image of his foot 1 inch from his nose was too much for me. It definitely wasn't sexy and didn't arouse me in any way. To top it off, shortly after his foul smelling foot was away from his face, he leaned forward to kiss me. I rejected him, entirely.

Tears

When I first moved to Los Angeles I was more active with online dating because I was trying to meet people. I met up with a guy who completely misrepresented himself by way of his image. Apparently he was a former male model. He had tear sheets posted with some familiar supermodels from the 90's. When he showed up, I could tell it was him, but of course he'd aged a bit. He was still handsome, but I wondered why he didn't have any recent images of himself. Against my better judgment I agreed to have dinner.

We walked down to a local restaurant and right off the bat I could tell he was the argumentative type. He would ask me my opinion about something and then he would debate my answer. That was a red flag. We ordered wine and after the first glass he began talking about his ex-girlfriend. He told me they'd been gardening and done some landscaping together on his house and how he can't even go outside without being reminded of her.

I started to drift away in his rambling and then I noticed he began to slowly drop his head with his face downward. I leaned forward to take a closer look and he was crying. I asked him if he was okay and he didn't answer. Then I asked if he was thinking about his ex-girlfriend and he said *YES*. Needless to say, that date ended abruptly and I never saw or heard from him again.

I know it's not you in the photo...

It's bad enough to use old photos of yourself for your online profile, but what about when someone uses a photo that is entirely someone else? On another online escapade I decided to meet a guy by the screen name of Antonio1970 for coffee. We'd been talking by phone for a couple of weeks. His profile said he was from Italy and had recently moved to the United States. He had an Italian accent, but I found it peculiar that when I would ask him to say certain things in Italian he would have to think about it as if it wasn't his first language.

Anyway, when I arrived to the coffee shop he was nowhere in sight. At first I felt like he was another flake. The only people I saw in he coffee shop were a woman and her child and a man wearing a baseball cap that looked nothing like Antonio. I went outside and called to see where he was and he said he was right in front of me. I looked and looked but still, no Antonio1970 in sight. A man walked up and introduced himself as the man I was looking for, but the Antonio1970 and the guy standing before me were not one and the same, he was the guy wearing the baseball cap.

I politely engaged in a brief, but awkward conversation and while saying good-bye I told him it was obvious he used someone else's photo. His only defense was, "I am a nice guy though." It wasn't enough that he actually believed that I either wouldn't notice or that it would be okay. I had no interest in finding out if he was a nice guy, I already knew he was deceitful and that was enough.

How about some testicles with dinner?

There is always that one bad date that can never be topped and here it is. It all started with yet again what seemed to be my never-ending ability to be duped by ones photos. I may have gotten duped so many times before, but at least I learned what to look out for. This one had a well-written profile with just enough humor. Of course his photos were a little unclear and in the ones that were clear he was standing very far away.

We engaged in a few nice emails and spoke on the phone a few times. There didn't seem to be any pressure in meeting. So I called him up to tell him that a friend of mine and I were going to be strolling through the area where his shop was and if he were okay with it we would just pop in to say hello. He was more than warm with the reception, but he didn't look anything like his photos. He was still pleasant however and invited my friend and I to dinner down the street. My friend was a guy from out of town who told me to give him a chance. What harm would it do right? After all, he didn't seem to be the jealous type and was very personable. I liked it.

I'm not a drinker, but I am totally comfortable having dinner with people who do. Half way through dinner he had polished off two bottles of wine with my friend. As I sat enjoying my meal I was barely listening to the conversation going on between my friend and my date. However, I couldn't help but over hear my date mention the word "testicles." I turned and looked at him and he said, *"Yes, I said testicles."* He then went ion about the elasticity of his friend's scrotum. Apparently, he was fascinated with how far a man could stretch his sack and thought we needed to be educated. His friend had the ability to stretch the skin from the lower section of his scrotum to the top so he could examine a "bump" and determine whether or not he had herpes. Mind you, this was our first date and we were at dinner. I went home and tried to process what had happened. Maybe it was he alcohol talking, maybe I made him nervous, and maybe my friend initiated the conversation, who knows. Just went I'd almost made a good excuse for his behavior he sends me a text at 1am that read, *Too much class will make you grow testicles.*" Followed by a text that read, *"Just thinking of you."* So, at 1am, I made him think about testicles?

The next morning I wrote to him online and told him how I felt about the conversation at dinner and by it being paired with a 1am text message made me certain he wasn't a match for me.

To this day, I still have not grown testicles.

Chapter V

Hate less and Love Always

Why the "good ones" hide

Many men and women deliver messages packed with personal and bitter diatribes for one another. Then they wonder why they can't find a "good one." The answer is simple, it's because the good ones are hiding, hiding from them. What caring and kindhearted person deserves or wants to be with someone who does nothing but offer words of bitterness and hatred towards them?

My daily banter would consist of living a good life accompanied by a poetic phrase of the demise of the quality in men of my generation. To no surprise, the change from bad to better within me did not occur over night and even after feeling good about my life, I still found myself chasing after dysfunctional men or those who did not want to be with me.

My behavior was typical of someone with fear of abandonment. There were three situations, which were direct sources of my abandonment issues. The first, being left by my mother when I was an infant. Though I wasn't able to process it until I became an adult, by my mother leaving I felt unloved and disregarded because of the parental bond a mother is supposed to have with her child. The second source of my abandonment issues was when my dad left me to live with my abusive grandmother. I felt the only person whom I trusted had thrown me to the wolves. Knowing he was well aware my grandmother harbored such hatred towards me, but still left me to endure such anguish made me resentful and left me confused.

When my dad passed away I felt abandoned for the third time. Obviously, his death was not an intentional abandonment, but nonetheless I still was left to feel alone, and deserted. I felt like my safety net had left me for good.

One of reasons I continued to date men who were emotionally unavailable like the cheaters and bad boys was because they would leave before I became attached to them, which decreased the chances of feeling the pain from being abandoned. How can someone leave you if they were never there to begin with? It made it much easier for me to divert attention away from the issues of having low self-esteem by portraying myself as a victim rather than having the self-worth to keep men like this out of my life to begin with. With others, I had a tendency to sabotage the relationship by behaving erratically to drive them away before they could get past my wall, because I that thought by letting them in, I would also be giving them an opportunity to leave.

Who would think someone who made you see so many different shades of red could end up being the catalyst for the change needed within? In 2007, I thought I'd met the devil himself and the king of all sociopaths. As usual there was something mysterious about his unavailability, which drew me to him. What I would come to find was that his unavailability to me was nothing more than it being because he was always available for other women, several other women. For both of us, it was the first thing we'd had even close to an actual steady relationship in years. Keep in mind, being steady just means you see each other steadily, it's not to be mistaken for being committed. Our relationship was intense and volatile, but even though it made me feel alive and like I was in an actual relationship, it brought about some of the most heartbreaking emotions I'd ever felt. We had an explosive breakup and though I felt as if there would be no end to the pain I felt,

I totally needed it. For once, I had actually fallen in love with someone. When things were good between us I felt as if I was complete. We could sit and talk for hours on end and our affection to one another was always welcomed. If it weren't for him I doubt I would have given a second thought to how I viewed life. It's like I needed to have that one ridiculously bad relationship to teach me something that I never knew before.

Having had troubles from his own childhood, he was able to find a way to maintain inner peace after reading The Power of Now by Eckhart Tolle. For Christmas he gave me a copy with a note written inside on how the book changed his life. I read the book and was able to understand it was my ego that held on to all the pain I had inside. I basically needed to get over myself! After several "ah hah" moments, I could feel my attitude and energy beginning to change. Unfortunately, his view of women could not be fixed by The Power of Now, but after our break up as strange as it was, he was remorseful. We decided to put the resentment aside and leave things on good terms. A year later we had dinner together. I hadn't seen him since we'd broken up, but I think we both felt like we needed some real closure. He had begun seeing someone and said he was faithful. He told me how his life and view of women had changed after I turned his world upside down and he thanked me. So basically, I fixed him for someone else. A bitter sweet ending I suppose, but as it stands, he turned out to be one of the few who wasn't a sociopath after all

Is what you see really what you get?

They say beauty is only skin deep and as I have been told I was a physically attractive girl for the longest time I felt I was the most hideous girl on the planet so the saying rings true. I didn't like people very much and I was a pessimistic and jealous girl with an elitist attitude. If you could think of the pretty girl who you wanted to fall in a mud puddle because of her sickening attitude, that was me. My misery showed in the company I kept as I surrounded myself with shallow people because they made being toxic acceptable.

Distorted Sense of Self

It only takes the approval of one person to instill a sense of entitlement to someone for the wrong reasons. If just one person laughs at an offensive joke, one might believe himself or herself to be a natural born comedian and they will continue to tell their tasteless jokes. If someone strikes another for any reason as long as there is someone to tell them they did the right thing because it was well deserved, they will continue to strike.

When I was that rude and unruly little girl I knew very well I was being obnoxious, but I didn't care. I had "friends" to back up my actions. I thought I was cool, because at some point someone said being spoiled was cute. After a while of seeing the sadness in their faces match mine, I began to feel guilty and ashamed. I had been projecting the way I felt about myself onto others the entire time.

I tried simply being polite or nice, but it was obvious that I needed to be more than that. I would do things to help others, but nothing was changing and I couldn't seem to wrap my head around why.

I had a friend jokingly tell me I had such a negative outlook at work one day and then later my boss told the same thing except he was serious; I realized there was some truth in what they were saying. I didn't necessarily look per se, but I would see the bad in most things; I always added "negatags" to everything. A "negatag" is simply a negative addition to a statement someone makes. For a minor example, if someone told me how much he or she was enjoying the day, I would say, "It would be better if it wasn't overcast." A major example would be when someone said something profound, I would subtract the importance of it and make it about something else and that something else was usually me.

My opinion of myself was that I had a positive attitude and a great outlook because I was a nice person, but sometimes being nice is simply nothing more than being well mannered; unfortunately, nice does not always mean you have a positive outlook.

Changing your outlook is not as easy as simply, "Looking for the good within others," many people claim to do that all the time. I took a different approach, one that worked for me. I made it a goal to challenge myself by remembering at least five good things a day and I immediately started noticing all the "nice" little things I took for granted, things like a genuine smile from a parking attendant and someone waving thank you for letting them cut in front of me during rush hour. To make it easier to see the good in life, get a sheet of paper and something to write with and simply make a list of how often people are nice to you. You will find that there are more pleasantries right in front of you that you'd never seen being focused on the bad things the world had to offer.

My outlook was one thing, opening my heart was another. Some believe that by simply being open to love it will find its way inside your heart; however, if you are holding in bitterness and anger, nothing can save you. Opening your heart serves two functions. You open it to release the negative emotions you are holding inside and you keep it open to allow love to come in.

It's like when a dam breaks, after the water comes spilling out, what's left is an open space that with enough light will allow a meadow to grow; after a flood of emotions, there is room for love to come in and enrich your soul. It took a lot of work, humility, and acceptance to open my heart, but when I did the flood of emotions came spilling out.

I can't emphasize enough on the importance of releasing the bitterness and anger caused from being hurt by others. It will not matter what you do to find romance, if you do not have a healthy attitude, nothing will fall into place as you desire.

Heartbreaker?

For me, rejecting someone was difficult for the fear of making a mistake or misjudging. However, after finally doing the work to make myself better I was able to separate reality from pessimism, I knew when I was setting myself up for an inevitable disappointment. It became easier to walk away when I felt like I deserved to be with what I wanted and that it was okay for me not to be interested.

When a person has nothing which interests you it's easy to reject them, but when you like something, even if it's just one tiny thing, is when the foolish optimism begins to start. You begin the process of trying to convince yourself "that little something" you like about them is better than it actually is. I've done this to avoid having to start the dating process over with someone else or to avoid being alone. Somehow we find ourselves taking bigger risks when we know someone wants us simply because it feels good to be wanted.

I have always attracted different types of men, from the deadbeats, to the ones to die for, as well as the "cubs," and those old enough to be my dad. The people we choose to date and associate with in general are a reflection of how we live our lives and how we truly feel about ourselves. When we surround ourselves with those who are self-destructive or who treat us poorly, we are revealed as one without self-love as we are choosing to allow the turmoil and chaos in our lives that keeps us submerged in pain and frustration.

Remaining friends and lovers of those who engage in underhanded practices says we approve and accept their behavior, thus we become the enabler. I went from being someone who always dated emotionally abusive or unavailable men; to the one who leaves without hesitation should there be signs of malicious behavior or ill intent. Choosing suitors based on who they are now and not what they have the potential to become keeps me from risking my state of being. It protects me from any sudden influxes of unhappiness, which would be caused by the hypothetical relationship I disguised as a fairy tale.

The Men Now

It's natural for physical attraction to be the first thing you notice about someone without knowing him or her. After all, you can't be attracted to someone's intelligence or know they have a good heart if you haven't a clue who they are. When I was younger I had a very distinguishable physical type, but as I get older it's more about compatibility than physical attraction or things we have in common.

I have found that I discover more suitable men by not searching for a type. When I had the checklist of things my ideal mate should have it turned out I was seeking perfection instead of just letting things be. Keep in mind, when I say to let things be, I'm not suggesting you take what's available just because it's before you.

When I meet men now, the only thing that crosses my mind when we speak is that I am interacting with a man. The question of whether or not he has potential to be my "once in a lifetime" is the farthest from my mind. By not romanticizing whether or not he could be "the one" takes the pressure off and I relax. People tend to be less intimidated by others who aren't tightly wound.

I don't consider this the approach of not setting yourself up for disappointment. For me, hoping for the best, but planning for the worst is only applicable if prepping for a natural disaster. If you apply it to everyday life and relationships you are anticipating disappointment or failure therefore, it will most likely happen. When the best doesn't happen it doesn't mean the result was the worst, it's just the outcome of whatever had taken place.

Happily ever after, until death I do part

From the moment we are able to comprehend our native language we are instilled with the belief we are supposed to fall in love, marry, and reproduce, often in this exact order. More than 80% of the entire population is religious with its own set of rules and guidelines when it comes to marriage.

Too often I have heard that I need a man in my life and the numbers of times my friends have tried to set me up with their "available" friends are too many to count. When I pulled myself away from the mind-set that I needed to be with someone to be complete was when I felt like I was truly living my life. Being the best human being I can be has given me what I need to live a fulfilled life and for the most part, I'm getting what I want out of life without many struggles.

Of course, the sense of belonging and coming home to someone has its good sides. It's nice to look forward to seeing someone and someone being there when you want to be in the company of another, but being single does not mean you're cursed. There is a sense of beauty in the freedom of being single. Being single gives you the freedom to do as you wish without being required to notify someone else and you don't have to deal with anyone else in your personal space unless you want to.

I'm single and happy, but this doesn't mean I'm happy because I'm single, it simply means I'm happy and my current relationship status is single. Therefore, if by chance someday I meet someone who suits me as a mate then I won't be single anymore, but I will still be happy. Being happy in life means I will be happy in any relationship that is a healthy one. I am finding that by being content makes it easier to identify and steer clear of unhealthy situations.

Life, love, and romance don't have to be complicated. It is often only chaotic and tangled when we make it that way. If love and being in a relationship is what you want, but your search is not quite turning out the way you had planned its time to step back to look at your situation. You can have both love and happiness without being married, without being "taken," and yes, you can have it being alone.

I got to a point in life when I asked myself a simple question: "Do I want to be happy or do I want to be miserable?" I chose happiness. The most simplistic way to look at it is by accepting that if you are a miserable person, you will definitely be miserable in a relationship because it is who you are. With misery you are more likely to repeat mistakes and continue to make bad decisions because you seek something or someone to "make" you happy instead of finding a way of "being" happy.

A state of happiness often generates a higher sense of self-worth naturally. The way you feel about yourself will show in your self-confidence and self-esteem, not only will this aid in making better decisions, it will also extend to everyday life situations like job interviews and conducting business.

When you are happy, you are content, and satisfied.

From Tenzin Gyatso: The Fourteenth Dalai Lama

"I believe that the purpose of life is to be happy. From the moment of birth, every human being wants happiness and does not want suffering. Neither social conditioning nor education nor ideology affects this. From the very core of our being, we simply desire contentment. I don't know whether the universe, with its countless galaxies, stars and planets, has a deeper meaning or not, but at the very least, it is clear that we humans who live on this earth face the task of making a happy life for ourselves. Therefore, it is important to discover what will bring about the greatest degree of happiness."

I am finally in that place where being around others and engaging in activities that bring me joy are a part of my daily routine, meaning being around good people and enjoying myself comes naturally. I don't seek things that make me happy; I am mostly in a constant state of happiness. However, being an inhabitant of this planet I have some days when I'm not as happy, but I don't consider myself to be having a "bad day."

You are entitled to love, to be loved and to live "happily ever after" with someone, but if it hasn't happened as soon as you'd hoped, or if it doesn't happen at all, it's not the end of the world. Do what you can to make your life one that is filled with all kinds of love and create joyous memories always, for when "death do you part," at least you can die smiling.

Acknowledgments

To Debra, my mentor, thank you for saving the world by helping me keep my sanity. I have learned so much from you about so many different things and most importantly I admire you for your will to be free from the obstacles life throws your way. You have been a major inspiration in my life.

Angie- I don't think I would have survived the drugs and alcohol long enough to write this book if it wasn't for my best friend. No matter how far apart or how much time goes by, we still speak the same. Thank you for keeping me alive and always being there, no matter how far you had to drive. I love you.

Luke- Special thanks to the one person who helped me get better by driving me mad. You are the only true ex-boyfriend I ever had; all the others were just guys I dated.

Rebecca-Finding courage within myself at such a young age kept me from settling for a life I would have never wanted, thank you for introducing me to spandex and Aqua Net, and showing me how to be courageous.

To Christy, thanks for always listening at any time during the day or during the week.

Josten Theney- thank-you for all your help and for being there without asking for anything in return.

It's not... the end.

www.ingramcontent.com/pod-product-compliance
Lightning Source LLC
Chambersburg PA
CBHW070643030426

42337CB00020B/4135